The Loving Heart

Copyright © 1992, Janette Oke

The Loving Heart

Published by Garborg's Heart 'n Home
P.O. Box 20132
Bloomington, MN 55420

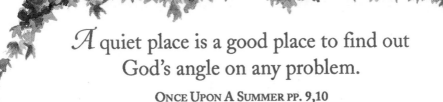

A quiet place is a good place to find out
God's angle on any problem.

ONCE UPON A SUMMER PP. 9,10

Think on these things.

PHILIPPIANS 4:8

∾∾∾∾∾∾∾∾∾∾∾∾∾∾∾

January 1

It is of the Lord's mercies that we are not consumed, because his compassions fail not. They are new every morning: great is thy faithfulness.

LAMENTATIONS 3:22,23

December 31

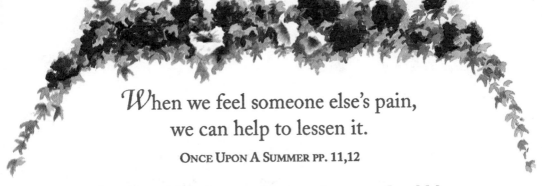

*W*hen we feel someone else's pain,
we can help to lessen it.

ONCE UPON A SUMMER PP. 11,12

*Comfort him, lest perhaps such a one should be
swallowed up with overmuch sorrow.*

2 CORINTHIANS 2:7

January 2

For he satisfieth the longing soul,
and filleth the hungry soul with goodness.

PSALM 107:9

~~~~~~~~~~~~~~~~

December 30

We will never regret doing the things
we know we should do.

ONCE UPON A SUMMER PP. 12,13

The statutes of the Lord are right,
rejoicing the heart.

PSALM 19:8

January 3

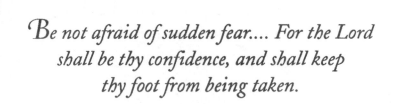

Be not afraid of sudden fear.... For the Lord shall be thy confidence, and shall keep thy foot from being taken.

PROVERBS 3:25,26

∽∽∽∽∽∽∽∽∽∽∽∽∽∽∽∽∽∽

December 29

No one ever outgrows the need for
a mother's love.

ONCE UPON A SUMMER PP. 13,14

Isaac was comforted after his mother's death.

GENESIS 24:67

∾∾∾∾∾∾∾∾∾∾∾∾∾∾∾

January 4

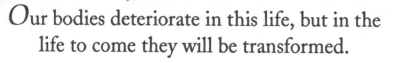

Our bodies deteriorate in this life, but in the life to come they will be transformed.

WHEN BREAKS THE DAWN PP. 101,102

We shall all be changed. For this corruptible must put on incorruption, and this mortal must put on immortality.

1 CORINTHIANS 15:52,53

December 28

If we savor the good times in youth, we can
enjoy them again in old age.

ONCE UPON A SUMMER PP.14,15

*They shall abundantly utter the memory
of thy great goodness.*

PSALM 145:7

January 5

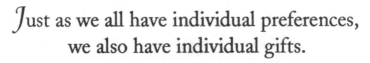

Just as we all have individual preferences,
we also have individual gifts.

WHEN BREAKS THE DAWN PP. 20-25

There are diversities of gifts, but the same Spirit.

1 CORINTHIANS 12:5

~ ~ ~ ~ ~ ~ ~ ~ ~ ~ ~ ~ ~ ~ ~ ~ ~

December 27

*U*gly feelings that we try to hide inside us
eventually surface as ugly behavior.

ONCE UPON A SUMMER PP. 15,16

He that covereth his sins shall not prosper.

PROVERBS 28:13

January 6

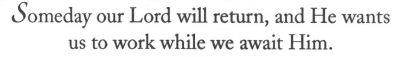

*S*omeday our Lord will return, and He wants
us to work while we await Him.

WHEN COMES THE SPRING PP. 212,213

Therefore be ye also ready: for in such an hour
as ye think not the Son of man cometh.

MATTHEW 24:44

∽∽∽∽∽∽∽∽∽∽∽∽∽∽∽∽∽∽∽

December 26

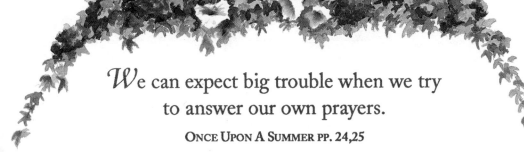

*W*e can expect big trouble when we try
to answer our own prayers.

ONCE UPON A SUMMER PP. 24,25

For your Father knows what you need
before you ask him.

MATTHEW 6:8

∾∾∾∾∾∾∾∾∾∾∾∾∾∾∾∾∾

January 7

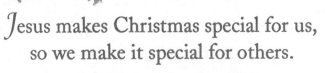

Jesus makes Christmas special for us,
so we make it special for others.

SPRING'S GENTLE PROMISE PP. 133,134

*Glory to God in the highest, and on earth
peace, good will toward men.*

LUKE 2:14

≈≈≈≈≈≈≈≈≈≈≈≈≈≈≈≈

December 25

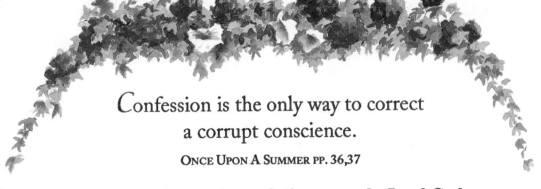

Confession is the only way to correct
a corrupt conscience.

ONCE UPON A SUMMER PP. 36,37

Now therefore make confession unto the Lord God.

EZRA 10:11

≈ ≈ ≈ ≈ ≈ ≈ ≈ ≈ ≈ ≈ ≈ ≈ ≈ ≈ ≈

January 8

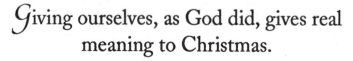

Giving ourselves, as God did, gives real
meaning to Christmas.

LOVE'S UNENDING LEGACY P. 83

Whosoever will be chief among you,
let him be your servant: Even as the Son of man
came not to be ministered unto, but to minister,
and to give his life a ransom for many.

MATTHEW 20:27,28

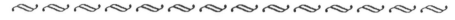

December 24

The blessing of an earthly family
gives us only a hazy picture of the blessing
in God's heavenly family.

ONCE UPON A SUMMER P. 72

*Children's children are the crown of old men; and the
glory of children are their fathers.*

PROVERBS 17:6

~~~~~~~~~~~~~~~~~

January 9

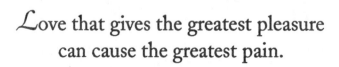

Love that gives the greatest pleasure
can cause the greatest pain.

LOVE'S ENDURING PROMISE P. 18

God so loved...that he gave his...Son.

JOHN 3:16

~~~~~~~~~~~~~~~~~~~~~~~~~

December 23

The changes in nature remind
us of the glorious transformation that's
coming for all believers.

ONCE UPON A SUMMER PP. 93,94

We shall all be changed.

1 CORINTHIANS 15:51

∽∽∽∽∽∽∽∽∽∽∽∽∽∽

January 10

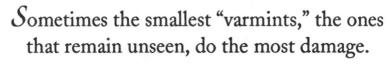

*S*ometimes the smallest "varmints," the ones that remain unseen, do the most damage.

WHEN CALLS THE HEART PP. 141-147

Who can understand his errors?
cleanse me from secret faults.

PSALM 19:12

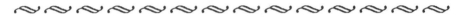

December 22

*W*hen our load is light, it's time
to carry someone else's.

ONCE UPON A SUMMER PP. 95,96

He is our help.

PSALM 33:20

≈≈≈≈≈≈≈≈≈≈≈≈≈≈≈≈

January 11

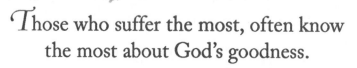

Those who suffer the most, often know
the most about God's goodness.

WHEN CALLS THE HEART PP. 128,129

Be not overcome of evil, but overcome evil with good.

ROMANS 12:21

~~~~~~~~~~~~~~~~~~~~~~~~~~~~~~~~~~

December 21

$\mathcal{W}$e never know which of the things we do
will stay forever in our minds, so it's best
to choose each action carefully.

ONCE UPON A SUMMER PP. 96,97

*O my God, my soul is cast down within me:
therefore will I remember thee.*

PSALM 42:6

January 12

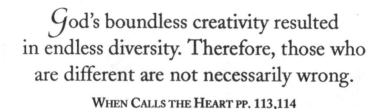

$\mathcal{G}$od's boundless creativity resulted
in endless diversity. Therefore, those who
are different are not necessarily wrong.

WHEN CALLS THE HEART PP. 113,114

If ye have respect to persons, ye commit sin.

JAMES 2:9

∽∽∽∽∽∽∽∽∽∽∽∽∽∽∽∽

December 20

*W*e do not always know the reasons
for what God does and doesn't do, but in the end
we'll see that He was always right.

ONCE UPON A SUMMER PP. 117,118

At the name of Jesus every knee should bow.

PHILIPPIANS 2:10

~~~~~~~~~~~~~~~~~

January 13

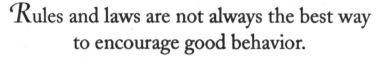

Rules and laws are not always the best way
to encourage good behavior.

WHEN CALLS THE HEART PP. 95,96

Ye have been called unto liberty;
only use not liberty for an occasion to the flesh,
but by love serve one another.

GALATIANS 5:13

December 19

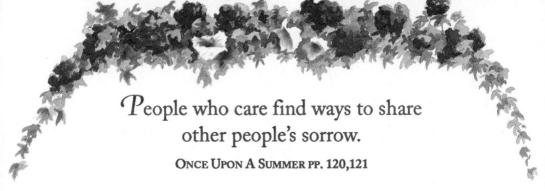

$\mathcal{P}$eople who care find ways to share
other people's sorrow.

ONCE UPON A SUMMER PP. 120,121

And went to him...and took care of him.

LUKE 10:34

~~~~~~~~~~~~~~~~~~~~~~

January 14

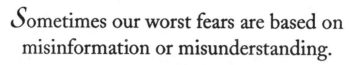

Sometimes our worst fears are based on misinformation or misunderstanding.

WHEN CALLS THE HEART PP. 79-83

But I will sing of thy power; yea, I will sing aloud of thy mercy in the morning; for thou hast been my defence and refuge in the day of my trouble.

PSAM 59:16

December 18

*W*rapping ourselves in bitterness is like using a blanket of poison ivy; it's warm at first but painful in the end.

ONCE UPON A SUMMER P. 122

Let all bitterness...be put away from you.

EPHESIANS 4:31

January 15

*H*ouses, weapons, and our own wits give us
an illusion of safety and help us feel secure,
but in the end, our only security is God.

WHEN CALLS THE HEART PP. 77,78

*Because of his strength will I wait upon thee:
for God is my defence.*

PSALM 59:9

December 17

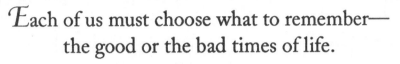

Each of us must choose what to remember—
the good or the bad times of life.

ONCE UPON A SUMMER PP. 122-124

I am full of heaviness: and I looked for some
to take pity, but there was none.

PSALM 69:20

January 16

It is wise to make provision for physical safety,
but it is even more important to make
provision for the safety of the soul.

WHEN CALLS THE HEART PP. 74-76

And fear not them which kill the body, but are not
able to kill the soul: but rather fear him which is
able to destroy both soul and body in hell.

MATTHEW 10:28

December 16

*H*ow we respond to hurt
determines whether our spirits will grow
and bloom or wither and die.

ONCE UPON A SUMMER PP.124,125

Having received the word in much affliction,
with joy of the Holy Ghost.

1 THESSALONIANS 1:6

~~~~~~~~~~~~~~~~~~~~~~~~~~~~~~

January 17

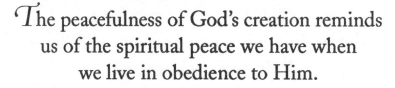

The peacefulness of God's creation reminds
us of the spiritual peace we have when
we live in obedience to Him.

WHEN CALLS THE HEART PP. 73,74

Great peace have they which love thy law:
and nothing shall offend them.

PSALM 119:165

～～～～～～～～～～～～～～～～～

December 15

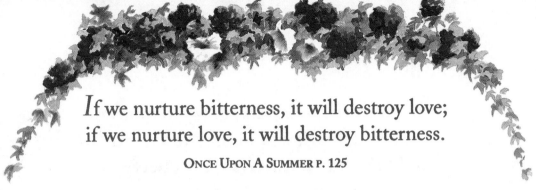

If we nurture bitterness, it will destroy love;
if we nurture love, it will destroy bitterness.

ONCE UPON A SUMMER P. 125

We are perplexed, but not in despair.

2 CORINTHIANS 4:8

~~~~~~~~~~~~~~~~~~~~~~~

January 18

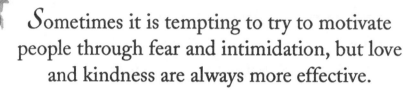

*S*ometimes it is tempting to try to motivate people through fear and intimidation, but love and kindness are always more effective.

WHEN CALLS THE HEART PP. 71,72

We love him, because he first loved us.

1 JOHN 4:19

~~~~~~~~~~~~~~~~~~~~~~

December 14

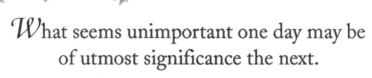

*W*hat seems unimportant one day may be
of utmost significance the next.

ONCE UPON A SUMMER PP. 146,147

*He is not here, but is risen: remember how he spake
unto you when he was yet in Galilee.*

LUKE 24:6

January 19

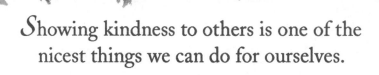

Showing kindness to others is one of the
nicest things we can do for ourselves.

WHEN CALLS THE HEART PP. 70,71

Be ye kind one to another, tenderhearted,
forgiving one another, even as God for
Christ's sake hath forgiven you.

EPHESIANS 4:32

December 13

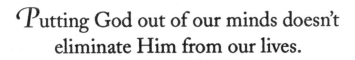

Putting God out of our minds doesn't
eliminate Him from our lives.

ONCE UPON A SUMMER PP. 147,148

Whither shall I go from thy spirit? or whither
shall I flee from thy presence?

PSALM 139:7

≈≈≈≈≈≈≈≈≈≈≈≈≈≈≈

January 20

*B*eing alone does not necessarily mean being lonely. In solitude we are more likely to hear God's sweetest songs.

WHEN CALLS THE HEART PP. 68,69

And when he had sent the multitudes away, he went up into a mountain apart to pray: and when the evening was come, he was there alone.

MATTHEW 14:23

December 12

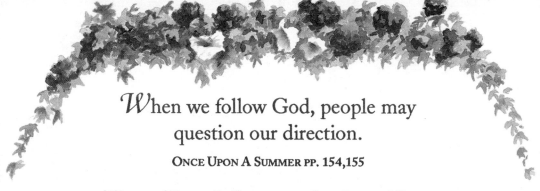

When we follow God, people may
question our direction.

ONCE UPON A SUMMER PP. 154,155

*They will not believe me...for they will say,
The Lord hath not appeared unto thee.*

EXODUS 4:1

~~~~~~~~~~~~~~~~~~~~~~~~~~~~

January 21

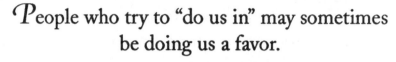

People who try to "do us in" may sometimes
be doing us a favor.

WHEN CALLS THE HEART PP. 60,61

*Ye thought evil against me; but God
meant it unto good.*

GENESIS 50:20

⁓ ⁓ ⁓ ⁓ ⁓ ⁓ ⁓ ⁓ ⁓ ⁓ ⁓ ⁓ ⁓ ⁓

December 11

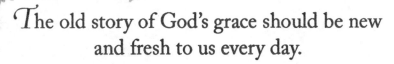

The old story of God's grace should be new
and fresh to us every day.

ONCE UPON A SUMMER PP. 159,160

And the grace of our Lord was exceeding abundant.

1 TIMOTHY 1:14

~~~~~~~~~~~~~~~~~~~~~

January 22

$\mathcal{F}$ear frequently accompanies new thoughts and ideas, but still we need to pursue them to determine whether or not they are for our good.

WHEN CALLS THE HEART PP. 16,17

But whoso hearkeneth unto me shall dwell safely,
and shall be quiet from fear of evil.

PROVERBS 1:33

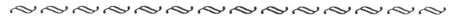

December 10

Confessing sin does more than just "patch up" our lives; it gives us a brand new start.

ONCE UPON A SUMMER PP. 163-165

I will confess my transgressions unto the Lord.

PSALM 32:5

≈≈≈≈≈≈≈≈≈≈≈≈≈≈≈

January 23

Children who learn spiritual truths early can be
trusted to make wise decisions as they grow older.

WHEN CALLS THE HEART PP. 15,16

*Train up a child in the way he should go: and when
he is old, he will not depart from it.*

PROVERBS 22:6

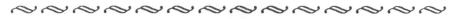

December 9

*W*hen our vision comes from God, there is no
doubt that we can accomplish it.

ONCE UPON A SUMMER PP. 165,166

*A vision appeared to Paul in the night;...saying, Come
over into Macedonia...immediately we endeavored to
go... assuredly gathering that the Lord had called us.*

ACTS 16:9,10

January 24

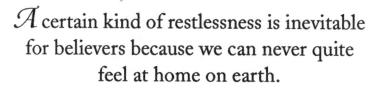

A certain kind of restlessness is inevitable
for believers because we can never quite
feel at home on earth.

WHEN CALLS THE HEART PP. 13,14

*We are confident, I say, and willing rather to be absent
from the body, and to be present with the Lord.*

PHILIPPIANS 4:12

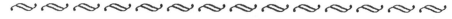

December 8

If we accept a rumor as fact, we encourage rumor spreaders, making it more likely that we too will become a victim of an untrue rumor.

ONCE UPON A SUMMER PP. 167,168

But let none of you suffer as...a busybody in other men's matters.

1 PETER 4:15

January 25

The happiest ending of all is when we are home
with the ones we love and the One who loves us.

LOVE FINDS A HOME PP. 217,218

Being rooted and grounded in love, may [you]
be able to comprehend...the love of Christ...that ye might
be filled with all the fulness of God.

EPHESIANS 3:17-19

December 7

Sowing seeds of doubt brings a harvest
of confusion, misunderstanding, and hurt.

ONCE UPON A SUMMER PP. 167-169

*And if I have taken any thing from any man
by false accusation, I restore him fourfold.*

LUKE 19:8

January 26

Giving to others what is rightfully ours is a good indication that we are following Christ's example.

LOVE FINDS A HOME PP. 191,192

Give, and it shall be given unto you; good measure, pressed down, and shaken together, and running over, shall men give into your bosom. With the same measure that ye mete withal it shall be measured to you again.

LUKE 6:38

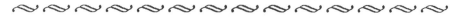

December 6

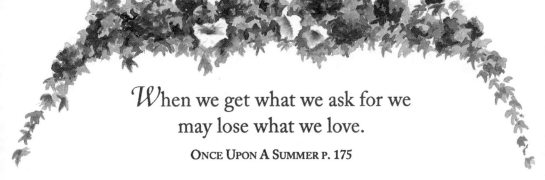

*W*hen we get what we ask for we
may lose what we love.

ONCE UPON A SUMMER P. 175

*We have added unto all our sins this
evil, to ask us a king.*

1 SAMUEL 12:19

~~~~~~~~~~~~~~~~~~~~~~~~~~~

January 27

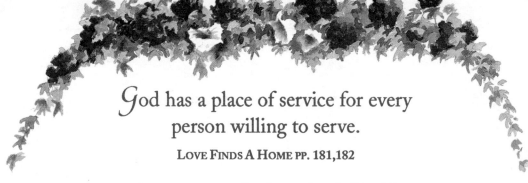

God has a place of service for every
person willing to serve.

LOVE FINDS A HOME PP. 181,182

As every man hath received the gift,
even so minister the same one to another, as good
stewards of the manifold grace of God.

1 PETER 4:10

December 5

*W*hen someone's good reputation needs
defending, it is not the time for silence.

ONCE UPON A SUMMER PP. 176,177

A time to keep silence, and a time to speak.

ECCLESIASTES 3:7

January 28

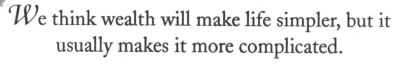

$\mathcal{W}$e think wealth will make life simpler, but it usually makes it more complicated.

LOVE FINDS A HOME PP. 168,169

He that trusteth in his riches shall fall: but the righteous shall flourish as a branch.

PROVERBS 11:28

December 4

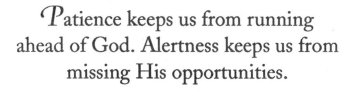

Patience keeps us from running
ahead of God. Alertness keeps us from
missing His opportunities.

ONCE UPON A SUMMER PP. 190-192

As we have therefore opportunity,
let us do good unto all men.

GALATIANS 6:10

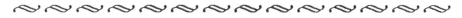

January 29

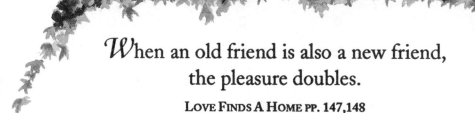

*W*hen an old friend is also a new friend,
the pleasure doubles.

LOVE FINDS A HOME PP. 147,148

A friend loveth at all times.

PROVERBS 17:17

≈≈≈≈≈≈≈≈≈≈≈≈≈≈≈

December 3

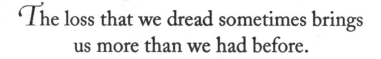

The loss that we dread sometimes brings
us more than we had before.

ONCE UPON A SUMMER P. 196

Thomas saith unto him, Lord,
we know not whither thou goest; and how
can we know the way?

JOHN 14:5

~~~~~~~~~~~~~~~~~~~~~~~~

January 30

We think that having more possessions will ease
our burdens, but it's more likely that the possessions
themselves will become a burden.

LOVE FINDS A HOME PP. 111,112

*Take heed, and beware of covetousness:
for a man's life consisteth not in the abundance
of the things which he possesseth.*

LUKE 12:15

December 2

I will praise thee, O Lord, with my whole heart; I will shew forth all thy marvellous works. I will be glad and rejoice in thee: I will sing praise to thy name, O thou most High.

PSALM 9:1,2

January 31

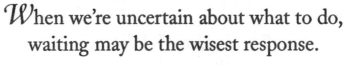

*W*hen we're uncertain about what to do,
waiting may be the wisest response.

LOVE FINDS A HOME pp. 104,105

Wait on the LORD: be of good courage,
and he shall strengthen thine heart:
wait, I say, on the LORD.

PSALM 27:14

December 1

*W*e all want peace, but few of us are willing
to give up our pride and self-ambition to get it.

ONCE UPON A SUMMER P. 198

We have an altar, whereof they have no right
to eat which serve the tabernacle.

HEBREWS 13:10

February 1

*And let us consider one another to provoke
unto love and to good works.*

HEBREWS 10:24

~~~~~~~~~~~~~~~~~~~~~~~~~~~~~

November 30

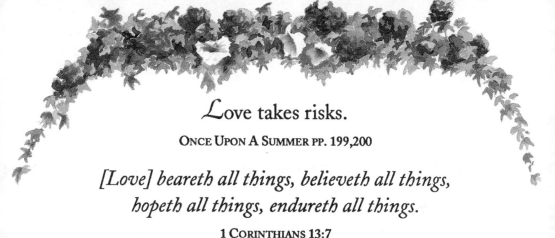

Love takes risks.

ONCE UPON A SUMMER PP. 199,200

*[Love] beareth all things, believeth all things,
hopeth all things, endureth all things.*

1 CORINTHIANS 13:7

∽∽∽∽∽∽∽∽∽∽∽∽∽∽∽∽∽

February 2

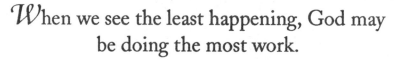

*W*hen we see the least happening, God may
be doing the most work.

LOVE FINDS A HOME PP. 93,94

O the depth of the riches both of the wisdom and
knowledge of God! how unsearchable are his judgments,
and his ways past finding out!

ROMANS 11:33

≈≈≈≈≈≈≈≈≈≈≈≈≈≈≈≈≈

November 29

Accepting God's love enables us to love others.

ONCE UPON A SUMMER PP. 200,201

Hereby perceive we the love of God,
because he laid down his life for us: and we ought
to lay down our lives for the brethren.

1 JOHN 3:16

≈≈≈≈≈≈≈≈≈≈≈≈≈≈≈≈

February 3

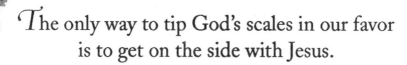

The only way to tip God's scales in our favor
is to get on the side with Jesus.

LOVE FINDS A HOME P. 93

*Jesus saith unto him, I am the way, the truth, and the
life: no man cometh unto the Father, but by me.*

JOHN 14:6

November 28

What we consider "bad luck" may be
part of God's sovereign plan.

THE WINDS OF AUTUMN PP. 60,61

The Lord maketh poor, and maketh rich:
he bringeth low, and lifteth up.

1 SAMUEL 2:7

February 4

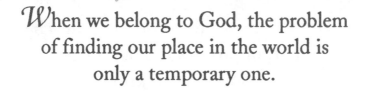

*W*hen we belong to God, the problem
of finding our place in the world is
only a temporary one.

LOVE FINDS A HOME PP. 84,85

*If any man trust to himself that he is Christ's,
let him of himself think this again, that, as he
is Christ's, even so are we Christ's.*

2 CORINTHIANS 10:7

~~~~~~~~~~~~~~~~~~

November 27

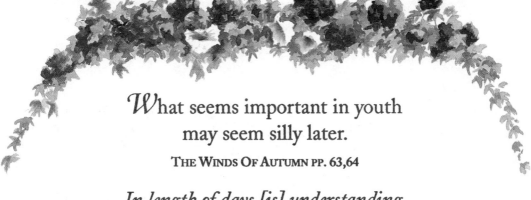

*W*hat seems important in youth
may seem silly later.

THE WINDS OF AUTUMN PP. 63,64

In length of days [is] understanding.

JOB 12:12

~~~~~~~~~~~~~~~~~~~~~~~~~

February 5

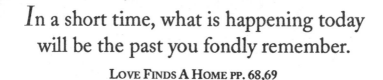

In a short time, what is happening today
will be the past you fondly remember.

LOVE FINDS A HOME PP. 68,69

*For I know the thoughts that I think toward you, saith
the LORD, thoughts of peace, and not of evil.*

JEREMIAH 29:11

November 26

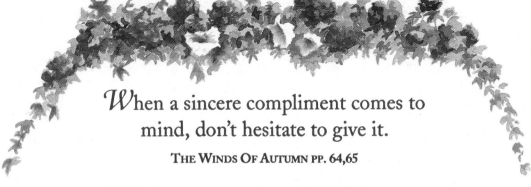

When a sincere compliment comes to
mind, don't hesitate to give it.

THE WINDS OF AUTUMN PP. 64,65

Well done, thou good and faithful servant.

MATTHEW 25:21

≈≈≈≈≈≈≈≈≈≈≈≈≈≈≈≈≈

February 6

*U*nimpressive people can make lasting
impressions with a simple act of kindness.

LOVE FINDS A HOME PP. 18,19

*But the fruit of the Spirit is love, joy, peace,
longsuffering, gentleness, goodness, faith.*

GALATIANS 5:22

~ ~ ~ ~ ~ ~ ~ ~ ~ ~ ~ ~ ~ ~ ~ ~

November 25

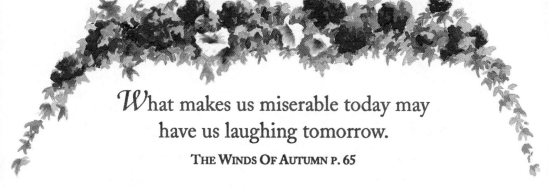

*W*hat makes us miserable today may
have us laughing tomorrow.

THE WINDS OF AUTUMN P. 65

*The Lord turned again the captivity of Zion....
Then was our mouth filled with laughter.*

PSALM 126:1,2

~~~~~~~~~~~~~~~~~~~~~

February 7

Satan doesn't always pursue us like a hunter with a deadly weapon; sometimes he lures us like a trout fisherman with an irresistible fly.

LOVE TAKES WING P. 218

But I fear...as the serpent beguiled Eve through subtilty, so your minds should be corrupted from the simplicity that is in Christ.

2 CORINTHIANS 11:3

~~~~~~~~~~~~~~~~~~~~~~~~~~~~~~~~~~~

November 24

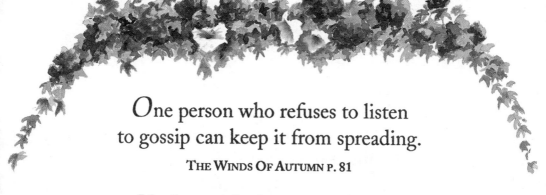

One person who refuses to listen
to gossip can keep it from spreading.

THE WINDS OF AUTUMN P. 81

*He that goeth about as a talebearer
revealeth secrets: therefore meddle not with
him that flattereth with his lips.*

PROVERBS 20:19

~~~~~~~~~~~~~~~~~~~~~~~~

February 8

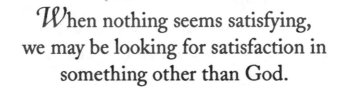

*W*hen nothing seems satisfying,
we may be looking for satisfaction in
something other than God.

LOVE TAKES WING PP. 216,217

*As for me, I will behold thy face in righteousness: I shall
be satisfied when I awake with thy likeness.*

PSALM 17:15

≈≈≈≈≈≈≈≈≈≈≈≈≈≈≈≈

November 23

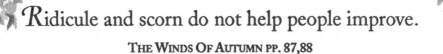

Ridicule and scorn do not help people improve.

THE WINDS OF AUTUMN PP. 87,88

*Speak evil of no man...shewing all
meekness unto all men.*

TITUS 3:2

∼∼∼∼∼∼∼∼∼∼∼∼∼∼∼∼

February 9

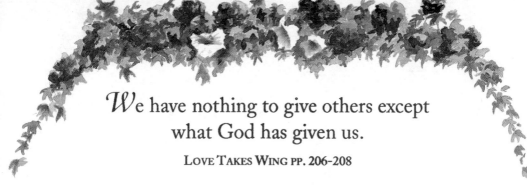

*W*e have nothing to give others except
what God has given us.

LOVE TAKES WING PP. 206-208

A man can receive nothing, except it be
given him from heaven.

JOHN 3:27

November 22

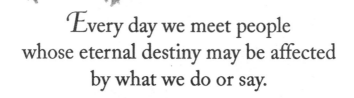

*E*very day we meet people
whose eternal destiny may be affected
by what we do or say.

THE WINDS OF AUTUMN PP. 99,100

Let every one of us please his neighbor
for his good to edification.

ROMANS 15:2

～～～～～～～～～～～～～～

February 10

Beauty outside is no guarantee of warmth inside.

LOVE TAKES WING PP. 173,174

We have a building of God, an house not made
with hands, eternal in the heavens.

2 CORINTHIANS 5:1

~~~~~~~~~~~~~~~~~~~~~~~~~~~~~~~

November 21

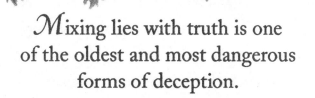

Mixing lies with truth is one
of the oldest and most dangerous
forms of deception.

THE WINDS OF AUTUMN PP. 112,113

The serpent...said unto the woman, Yea, hath God said,
Ye shall not eat of every tree of the garden?

GENESIS 3:1

~~~~~~~~~~~~~~~~~~~~~~~~~~~~~~~~~

February 11

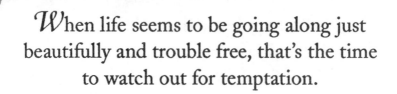

*W*hen life seems to be going along just
beautifully and trouble free, that's the time
to watch out for temptation.

LOVE TAKES WING PP.151-157

Watch ye and pray, lest ye enter into temptation.

MARK 14:38

November 20

It is dangerous to get close to those
who are far from God.

THE WINDS OF AUTUMN PP. 114-118

*Blessed is the man that walketh not
in the counsel of the ungodly.*

PSALM 1:1

～～～～～～～～～～～～～～～～

February 12

A heavy heart weighs more than
any other burden.

LOVE TAKES WING PP. 145,146

First, cast the beam out of thine own eye;
and then shalt thou see clearly to cast the mote
out of thy brother's eye.

MATTHEW 7:5

~~~~~~~~~~~~~~~~~~~~~~~~~~~~~~

November 19

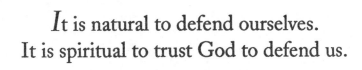

It is natural to defend ourselves.
It is spiritual to trust God to defend us.

THE WINDS OF AUTUMN PP. 119,120

*Unto him that smiteth thee
on the one cheek offer also the other.*

LUKE 6:29

∽∽∽∽∽∽∽∽∽∽∽∽∽∽∽∽∽

February 13

*H*uman effort can bring people
together physically, but only God's effort
can bring them together spiritually.

LOVE TAKES WING PP. 137,138

*If we walk in the light, as he is in the light,
we have fellowship one with another.*

1 JOHN 1:7

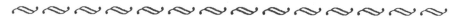

November 18

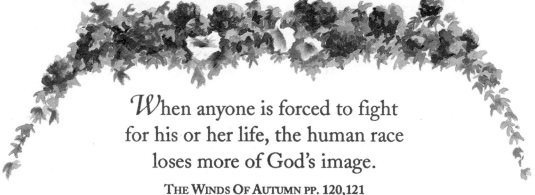

*W*hen anyone is forced to fight
for his or her life, the human race
loses more of God's image.

THE WINDS OF AUTUMN PP. 120,121

*Bless them that curse you, and pray for
them which despitefully use you.*

LUKE 6:28

February 14

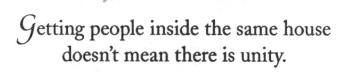

Getting people inside the same house
doesn't mean there is unity.

LOVE TAKES WING PP. 98,99

*How good and how pleasant it is for brethren
to dwell together in unity!*

PSALM 133:1

November 17

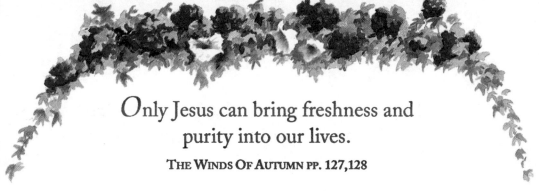

Only Jesus can bring freshness and
purity into our lives.

THE WINDS OF AUTUMN PP. 127,128

Wash me, and I shall be whiter than snow.

PSALM 51:7

≈≈≈≈≈≈≈≈≈≈≈≈≈≈≈≈≈

February 15

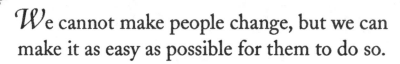

*W*e cannot make people change, but we can make it as easy as possible for them to do so.

LOVE TAKES WING PP. 97,98

If a man be overtaken in a fault...restore such an one in the spirit of meekness.

GALATIANS 6:1

November 16

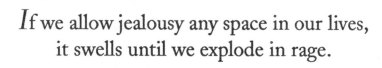

If we allow jealousy any space in our lives,
it swells until we explode in rage.

THE WINDS OF AUTUMN PP. 128,129

Jealousy is the rage of a man.

PROVERBS 6:34

∽∽∽∽∽∽∽∽∽∽∽∽∽∽∽∽

February 16

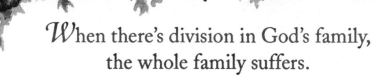

When there's division in God's family,
the whole family suffers.

LOVE TAKES WING PP. 95,96

*I beseech you, brethren, by the name of our Lord Jesus
Christ, that ye all speak the same thing, and that there
be no divisions among you; but that ye be perfectly joined
together in the same mind and in the same judgement.*

1 CORINTHIANS 1:10

November 15

The mystery and miracle of the
incarnation makes every day a Christmas
celebration for the believer.

THE WINDS OF AUTUMN PP. 133,134

I bring you good tidings of great joy,
which shall be to all people.

LUKE 2:10

⤳⤳⤳⤳⤳⤳⤳⤳⤳⤳⤳⤳⤳⤳⤳⤳⤳⤳

February 17

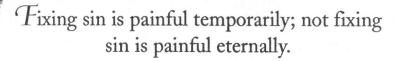

Fixing sin is painful temporarily; not fixing
sin is painful eternally.

LOVE TAKES WING P. 85

*No chastening for the present seemeth
to be joyous, but grievous: nevertheless afterward it
yieldeth the peaceable fruit of righteousness unto
them which are exercised thereby.*

HEBREWS 12:11

∾ ∾ ∾ ∾ ∾ ∾ ∾ ∾ ∾ ∾ ∾ ∾ ∾ ∾ ∾ ∾

November 14

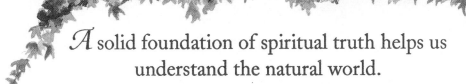

$\mathcal{A}$ solid foundation of spiritual truth helps us understand the natural world.

THE WINDS OF AUTUMN PP. 145,146

The natural man receiveth not the things of the Spirit of God.

1 CORINTHIANS 2:14

∽∽∽∽∽∽∽∽∽∽∽∽∽∽∽∽

February 18

$\mathcal{T}$ime seems to go faster the older we get because
each additional year is a smaller percentage
of the total time we have lived.

LOVE TAKES WING PP.42,43,73,74

I have been young, and now am old;
yet have I not seen the righteous forsaken.

PSALM 37:25

~~~~~~~~~~~~~~~~~~~~~~~~~~~~~~~~~~~~

November 13

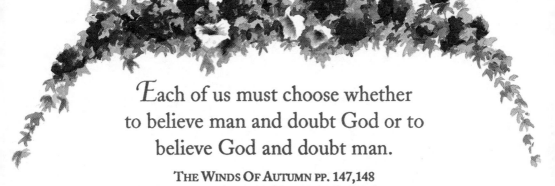

Each of us must choose whether
to believe man and doubt God or to
believe God and doubt man.

THE WINDS OF AUTUMN PP. 147,148

Who hath known the mind of the Lord,
that he may instruct him.

1 CORINTHIANS 2:16

February 19

Confidence in ourselves begins
with confidence in God.

LOVE'S UNFOLDING DREAM PP. 218-221

*This is the confidence that we have in him, that, if we
ask any thing according to his will, he heareth us.*

1 JOHN 5:14

≈≈≈≈≈≈≈≈≈≈≈≈≈≈≈

November 12

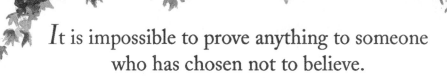

It is impossible to prove anything to someone
who has chosen not to believe.

THE WINDS OF AUTUMN PP. 148,149

*Who changed the truth of God into a lie, and
worshipped...the creature more than the Creator....*

ROMANS 1:25

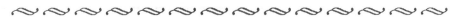

February 20

*I*t is impossible to lose our bitterness
without finding God first.

LOVE'S UNFOLDING DREAM PP. 209-214

*I love them that love me; and those that
seek me early shall find me.*

PROVERBS 8:17

November 11

Being open-minded is like driving a convertible;
it's great under certain conditions, but if you don't
know when to put the top on you'll be all wet.

THE WINDS OF AUTUMN PP.152,153

And ye shall know the truth, and the
truth shall make you free.

JOHN 8:32

February 21

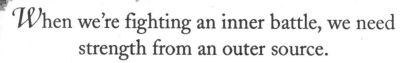

*W*hen we're fighting an inner battle, we need
strength from an outer source.

LOVE'S UNFOLDING DREAM PP. 206,207

My strength is made perfect in weakness.

2 CORINTHIANS 12:9

∽∽∽∽∽∽∽∽∽∽∽∽∽∽∽

November 10

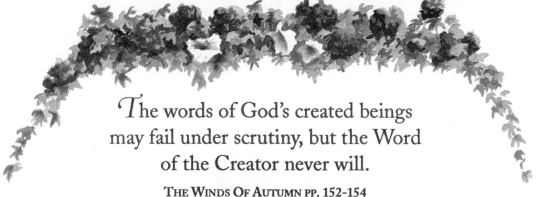

The words of God's created beings
may fail under scrutiny, but the Word
of the Creator never will.

THE WINDS OF AUTUMN PP. 152-154

Heaven and earth shall pass away, but my
words shall not pass away.

MATTHEW 24:35

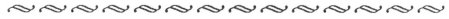

February 22

*I*f we spend more time taking care
of what we have and less time wanting what
we don't have, we might find out that we
already have what we want.

LOVE'S UNFOLDING DREAM PP. 197,198

*O fear the LORD, ye his saints: for there is no
want to them that fear him.... They that seek the LORD
shall not want any good thing.*

PSALM 34:9,10

≈ ≈ ≈ ≈ ≈ ≈ ≈ ≈ ≈ ≈ ≈ ≈ ≈ ≈

November 9

*I*t is better to be strangers than
friends separated by sin.

THE WINDS OF AUTUMN PP. 161,162

Make no friendship with an angry man.

PROVERBS 22:24

~~~~~~~~~~~~~~~~~~~~~~~~~~~~~

February 23

*W*e need not be any more reluctant
to accept charity when we need it than we
are to give it when others need it.

LOVE'S UNFOLDING DREAM P. 197

And all that believed were together, and had
all things common; and sold their possessions and goods,
and parted them to all men, as every man had need.

ACTS 2:44,45

November 8

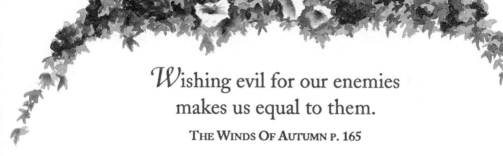

*W*ishing evil for our enemies
makes us equal to them.

THE WINDS OF AUTUMN P. 165

*Rejoice not when thine enemy falleth,
and let not thine heart be glad when he stumbleth.*

PROVERBS 24:17

~~~~~~~~~~~~~~~

February 24

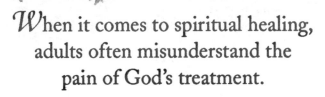

When it comes to spiritual healing,
adults often misunderstand the
pain of God's treatment.

LOVE'S UNFOLDING DREAM PP. 183, 184

*Think it not strange concerning the fiery trial
which is to try you.... But rejoice, inasmuch as ye
are partakers of Christ's suffering.*

1 PETER 4:12,13

~~~~~~~~~~~~~~~~~~~~~~~~~~

November 7

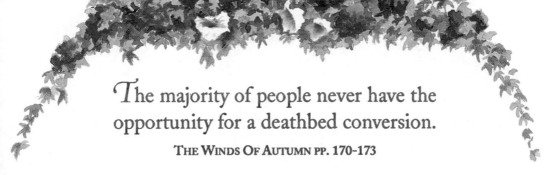

The majority of people never have the
opportunity for a deathbed conversion.

THE WINDS OF AUTUMN PP. 170-173

Now is the day of salvation.

2 CORINTHIANS 6:2

~~~~~~~~~~~~~~~~~~~~~~~~~~~~~

February 25

If we don't make poor people feel welcome,
maybe our standards are different from God's.

LOVE'S UNFOLDING DREAM P. 165

The LORD will maintain the cause of the afflicted,
and the right of the poor.

PSALM 140:12

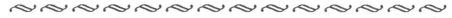

November 6

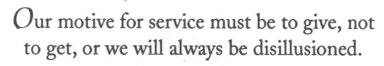

Our motive for service must be to give, not to get, or we will always be disillusioned.

THE WINDS OF AUTUMN PP. 174,175

With good will doing service, as to the Lord, and not to men.

EPHESIANS 6:7

~~~~~~~~~~~~~~~~~~~~~~~

February 26

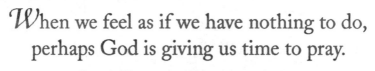

*W*hen we feel as if we have nothing to do,
perhaps God is giving us time to pray.

LOVE'S UNFOLDING DREAM PP. 158-161

*The effectual fervent prayer of a righteous
man availeth much.*

JAMES 5:16

November 5

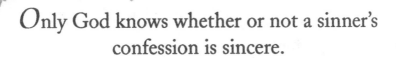

Only God knows whether or not a sinner's
confession is sincere.

THE WINDS OF AUTUMN PP. 176,177

Not everyone that saith unto me, Lord, Lord, shall enter
the Kingdom of heaven.

MATTHEW 7:21

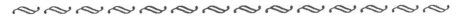

February 27

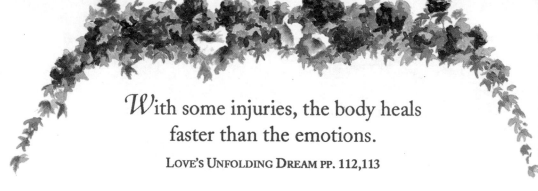

With some injuries, the body heals
faster than the emotions.

LOVE'S UNFOLDING DREAM PP. 112,113

He healeth the broken in heart, and
bindeth up their wounds.

PSALM 147:3

November 4

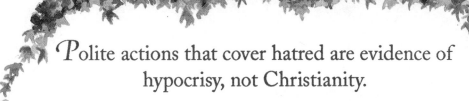

Polite actions that cover hatred are evidence of
hypocrisy, not Christianity.

THE WINDS OF AUTUMN PP. 180,181

It was not an enemy that reproached me;
then I could have borne it.

PSALM 55:12

February 28

Unrealistic expectations may lead to
unexpected disappointment.

LOVE'S UNFOLDING DREAM PP. 87,88

*And [Jesus] cometh, and findeth them sleeping,
and saith unto Peter, Simon, sleepest thou?
Couldest not thou watch one hour?*

MARK 14:37

≈≈≈≈≈≈≈≈≈≈≈≈≈≈≈≈

November 3

Without counsel purposes are disappointed: but in the multitude of counsellors they are established.

PROVERBS 15:22

❧❧❧❧❧❧❧❧❧❧❧❧❧❧❧❧❧

February 29

*W*hen we pay close attention to our children's strengths and weaknesses, we are better able to "train them in the way they should go."

LOVE'S UNFOLDING DREAM PP. 58,59

Train up a child in the way he should go: and when he is old, he will not depart from it.

PROVERBS 22:6

November 2

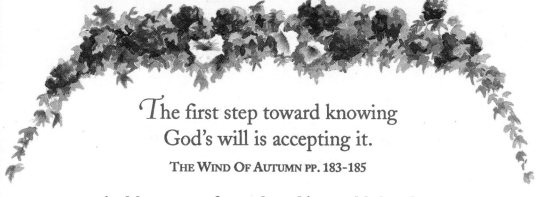

The first step toward knowing
God's will is accepting it.

THE WIND OF AUTUMN PP. 183-185

*And be not conformed to this world: but be ye
transformed by the renewing of your mind.*

ROMANS 12:2

~~~~~~~~~~~~~~~~~~~~~~~~

March 1

*W*hen our concern is genuine,
the fear of being misunderstood shouldn't
keep us from expressing it.

LOVE'S UNFOLDING DREAM PP. 43,44

*Be ye all of one mind, having compassion
one of another.*

1 PETER 3:8

November 1

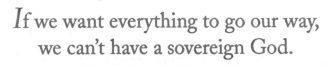

If we want everything to go our way,
we can't have a sovereign God.

THE WINDS OF AUTUMN PP. 185,186

*And [Jesus] said, Abba, Father, all things are possible
unto thee; take away this cup from me: nevertheless
not what I will, but what thou wilt.*

MARK 14:36

March 2

*Every good gift and every perfect gift
is from above, and cometh down from the Father
of lights, with whom is no variableness,
neither shadow of turning.*

JAMES 1:17

∽∽∽∽∽∽∽∽∽∽∽∽∽∽∽

October 31

*I*f our friends don't know God better for having
known us, we are not a good friend.

THE WINDS OF AUTUMN PP. 191,192

*Paul, an apostle of Jesus Christ by
the commandment of God our Saviour, and
Lord Jesus Christ, which is our hope.*

1 TIMOTHY 1:1

∾ ∾ ∾ ∾ ∾ ∾ ∾ ∾ ∾ ∾ ∾ ∾ ∾ ∾ ∾

March 3

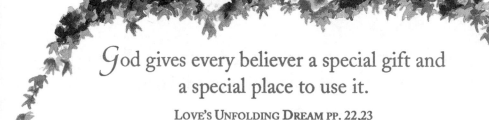

God gives every believer a special gift and
a special place to use it.

LOVE'S UNFOLDING DREAM PP. 22,23

*We, being many, are one body in Christ, and every one
members one of another. Having...gifts differing
according to the grace that is given to us.*

ROMANS 12:5,6

October 30

*W*hen it comes to understanding
the origin of the earth, we must have faith
in someone—God or man.

THE WINDS OF SUMMER PP. 192,193

*It is better to trust in the Lord than
to put confidence in man.*

PSALM 118:8

～～～～～～～～～～～～～～～

March 4

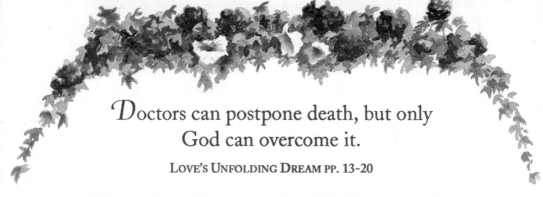

Doctors can postpone death, but only
God can overcome it.

LOVE'S UNFOLDING DREAM PP. 13-20

*He that heareth my word, and believeth on him
that sent me, hath everlasting life.*

JOHN 5:24

October 29

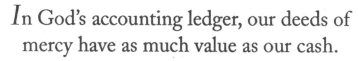

In God's accounting ledger, our deeds of
mercy have as much value as our cash.

THE WINDS OF AUTUMN PP. 193,194

*I beseech you therefore, brethren, by the mercies of God,
that ye present your bodies a living sacrifice, holy,
acceptable unto God, which is your reasonable service.*

ROMANS 12:1

March 5

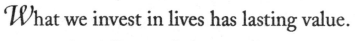

*W*hat we invest in lives has lasting value.

LOVE'S UNENDING LEGACY PP. 221-224

And these words...shall be in thine heart: and thou shalt teach them diligently unto thy children.

DEUTERONOMY 6:6,7

October 28

*W*e cannot be forgiven if we refuse to forgive.

THE WINDS OF AUTUMN PP. 195-197

But if ye forgive not men their trespasses,
neither will your Father forgive your trespasses.

MATTHEW 6:15

~~~~~~~~~~~~~~~~~~~~~~~~~~~~~~~

March 6

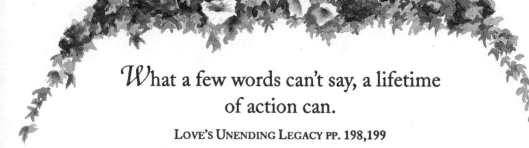

What a few words can't say, a lifetime
of action can.

LOVE'S UNENDING LEGACY PP. 198,199

Let us not love in word, neither in tongue;
but in deed and in truth.

1 JOHN 3:18

≈≈≈≈≈≈≈≈≈≈≈≈≈≈≈≈≈

October 27

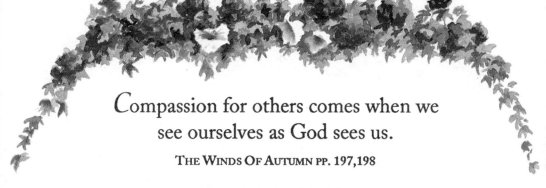

Compassion for others comes when we
see ourselves as God sees us.

THE WINDS OF AUTUMN PP. 197,198

*By mercy and truth iniquity is purged: and by
the fear of the Lord men depart from evil.*

PROVERBS 16:6

∽∽∽∽∽∽∽∽∽∽∽∽∽∽∽

March 7

Instead of crying over what has been taken *from* us, we should consider what has been given *to* us.

LOVE'S UNENDING LEGACY PP. 165,166

In everything give thanks: for this is the will of God in Christ Jesus concerning you.

1 THESSALONIANS 5:18

October 26

$\mathcal{D}$eath is frightening only
because we know more about the
physical world than the spiritual world.

THE WINDS OF AUTUMN PP. 200,201

*Yea, though I walk through the valley of the shadow
of death, I will fear no evil: for thou art with me.*

PSALM 23:4

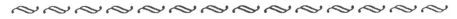

March 8

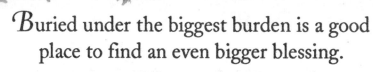

Buried under the biggest burden is a good
place to find an even bigger blessing.

LOVE'S UNENDING LEGACY PP. 151,152

*By the sadness of the countenance
the heart is made better.*

ECCLESIASTES 7:3

October 25

To feel love gives pleasure to one; to express it gives pleasure to two.

THE WINDS OF AUTUMN PP. 201,202

That their hearts might be comforted, being knit together in love.

COLOSSIANS 2:2

March 9

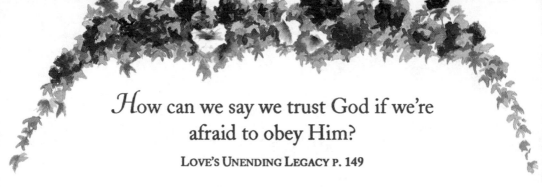

*H*ow can we say we trust God if we're
afraid to obey Him?

LOVE'S UNENDING LEGACY P. 149

Trust in the LORD, and do good.

PSALM 37:3

~~~~~~~~~~~~~~~~~~~~~~~~~~~~~~~

October 24

*H*arboring hate and bitterness is like spending
a whole inheritance on vinegar.

THE WINDS OF AUTUMN PP. 202,203

*And not many days after the younger son gathered all
together, and took his journey into a far country, and
there wasted his substance with riotous living.*

LUKE 15:13

March 10

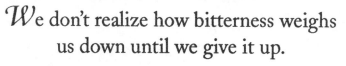

*W*e don't realize how bitterness weighs
us down until we give it up.

LOVE'S UNENDING LEGACY P. 148

Follow peace with all men, and holiness...
lest any root of bitterness springing up trouble you,
and thereby many be defiled.

HEBREWS 12:14,15

October 23

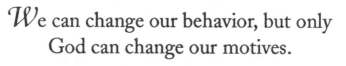

*W*e can change our behavior, but only
God can change our motives.

THE WINDS OF AUTUMN P. 206

*This people draweth nigh unto me with
their mouth, and honoureth me with their lips;
but their heart is far from me.*

MATTHEW 15:8

March 11

*W*hen our idea of perfection comes from God,
we don't pay much attention to appearance.

LOVE'S UNENDING LEGACY PP. 147,178

Be ye therefore perfect, even as your Father
which is in heaven is perfect.

MATTHEW 5:48

October 22

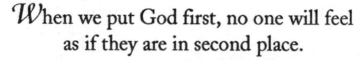

$\mathcal{W}$hen we put God first, no one will feel
as if they are in second place.

THE WINDS OF AUTUMN PP. 206,207

*But seek ye first the kingdom
of God, and his righteousness; and all
these things shall be added unto you.*

MATTHEW 6:33

March 12

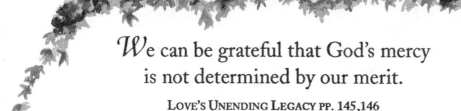

We can be grateful that God's mercy
is not determined by our merit.

LOVE'S UNENDING LEGACY PP. 145,146

*Not by works of righteousness which we have done,
but according to his mercy he saved us.*

TITUS 3:5

October 21

*H*ow we leave the world is
more important than how we enter it.

THE WINDS OF AUTUMN PP. 207,208

Being born again, not of corruptible
seed, but of incorruptible, by the word of God,
which liveth and abideth for ever.

1 PETER 1:23

~~~~~~~~~~~~~~~~~~~~~~~~~~~~~

March 13

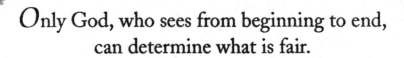

Only God, who sees from beginning to end,
can determine what is fair.

LOVE'S UNENDING LEGACY P. 143

Shall mortal man be more just than God?

JOB 4:17

∽∽∽∽∽∽∽∽∽∽∽∽∽∽∽∽∽

October 20

Scientists have only the past on which to base
their beliefs; with God, we have the future as well.

THE WINDS OF AUTUMN PP. 208,209

I am Alpha and Omega, the beginning
and the end, the first and the last.

REVELATION 22:13

∽∽∽∽∽∽∽∽∽∽∽∽∽∽∽∽

March 14

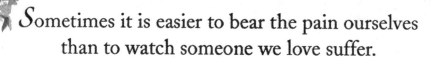

Sometimes it is easier to bear the pain ourselves
than to watch someone we love suffer.

LOVE'S UNENDING LEGACY P. 139

O my son Absolam,...would God I had died for thee!

2 SAMUEL 18:33

～～～～～～～～～～～～～～～～～～

October 19

*W*hen we pray with selfish
motives we are asking God to do our will
instead of surrendering to His.

THE WINDS OF AUTUMN PP. 209,210

Ye ask, and receive not, because ye ask amiss,
that ye may consume it upon your lusts.

JAMES 4:3

March 15

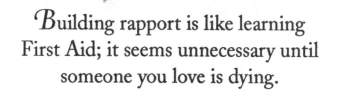

Building rapport is like learning
First Aid; it seems unnecessary until
someone you love is dying.

LOVE'S UNENDING LEGACY PP. 130,131

*Do good...ready to distribute,
willing to communicate; Laying up in store...
a good foundation against the time to come.*

1 TIMOTHY 6:18,19

∾ ∾ ∾ ∾ ∾ ∾ ∾ ∾ ∾ ∾ ∾ ∾ ∾ ∾ ∾ ∾

October 18

*W*hen our lives are full of what we want,
we have no room for what God wants to give us.

THE WINDS OF AUTUMN PP. 208-212

*Jesus said...Go and sell that thou hast, and give to the
poor, and thou shalt have treasure in heaven: and come
and follow me. When the young man heard that saying,
he went away sorrowful: for he had great possessions.*

MATTHEW 19:21,22

March 16

The closer we are to something,
the less we see of it. Only from God's
perspective is everything seen.

LOVE'S UNENDING LEGACY PP. 123,124

For now we see through a glass, darkly;
but then face to face: now I know in part; but then
shall I know even as I am known.

1 CORINTHIANS 13:12

~~~~~~~~~~~~~~~~~~~~~~~~

October 17

*G*rief is inevitable and painful, but for the Christians it is only temporary.

THE WINDS OF AUTUMN PP. 214,215

The righteous hath hope in his death.

PROVERBS 14:32

~~~~~~~~~~~~~~~~~~~~~~~

March 17

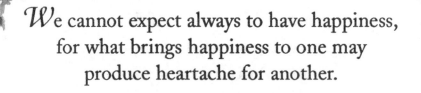

$\mathcal{W}$e cannot expect always to have happiness,
for what brings happiness to one may
produce heartache for another.

LOVE'S UNENDING LEGACY PP. 118,119

*Shall we receive good at the hand of God,
and shall we not receive evil?*

JOB 2:10

∾ ∾ ∾ ∾ ∾ ∾ ∾ ∾ ∾ ∾ ∾ ∾ ∾ ∾ ∾ ∾

October 16

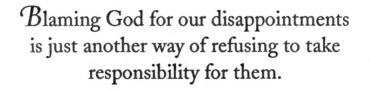

Blaming God for our disappointments
is just another way of refusing to take
responsibility for them.

THE WINDS OF AUTUMN PP. 215,216

*And it shall come to pass, that when
they shall be hungry, they shall fret themselves,
and curse their king and their God.*

ISAIAH 8:21

~~~~~~~~~~~~~~~~~~~~~~~~~~

March 18

Though only God's love can fulfill our deepest needs, the love between a man and woman can be an important part of God's plan for our lives.

WHEN CALLS THE HEART PP. 216-221

And the Lord God said, It is not good that the man should be alone; I will make him an help meet for him.

GENESIS 2:18,24

~~~~~~~~~~~~~~~~~~~~~

October 15

Surrendering to God gives us compassion
for those who have not yet done so.

THE WINDS OF AUTUMN P. 216

Be of the same mind toward another.
Mind not high things, but condescend to men
of low estate. Be not wise in your own conceits.

ROMANS 12:16

March 19

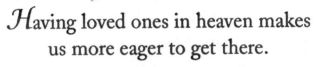

*H*aving loved ones in heaven makes
us more eager to get there.

LOVE'S UNENDING LEGACY P. 67

*In my Father's house are many mansions.... I go and
prepare a place for you, I will come again, and receive
you unto myself; that where I am, there ye may be also.*

JOHN 14: 2,3

October 14

Letting go of earthly attachments is the
only way to hold onto God.

THE WINDS OF AUTUMN P. 117

Father, into thy hands I commend my spirit.

LUKE 23:46

March 20

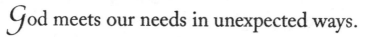

God meets our needs in unexpected ways.

LOVE'S UNENDING LEGACY PP. 43–45

Sarah conceived, and bare Abraham a son in his old age.... And Sarah said, God hath made me to laugh, so that all that hear will laugh with me.

GENESIS 21:2,6

October 13

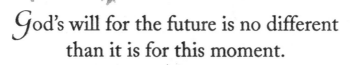

$\mathcal{G}$od's will for the future is no different
than it is for this moment.

WINTER IS NOT FOREVER PP. 13,14

A time to be born, and a time to die; a time to plant,
and a time to pluck up that which is planted.

ECCLESIASTES 3:2

$\mathcal{M}$arch 21

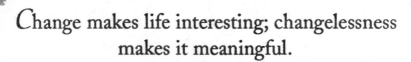

Change makes life interesting; changelessness
makes it meaningful.

Love's Unending Legacy pp. 28,29

He changeth the times and the seasons....
I am the LORD, I change not.

Daniel 2:21; Malachi 3:6

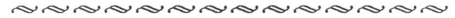

October 12

Physical freedom sometimes brings uncertainty; spiritual freedom always brings certainty.

WINTER IS NOT FOREVER P. 14

If the Son therefore shall make you free,
ye shall be free indeed.

JOHN 8:36

March 22

The only way to take control is to give it up.

LOVE'S UNENDING LEGACY P. 17

Whosoever will lose his life for my sake shall find it.

MATTHEW 16:25

~~~~~~~~~~~~~~~~

October 11

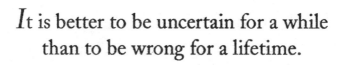

*I*t is better to be uncertain for a while
than to be wrong for a lifetime.

WINTER IS NOT FOREVER P. 27

And thy life shall hang in doubt before
thee; and thou shalt fear day and night, and
shalt have none assurance of thy life.

DEUTERONOMY 28:66

March 23

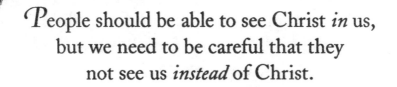

*P*eople should be able to see Christ *in* us,
but we need to be careful that they
not see us *instead* of Christ.

LOVE'S ABIDING JOY PP. 201,202

*I am crucified with Christ: nevertheless I live;
yet not I, but Christ liveth in me.*

GALATIANS 2:20

October 10

$\mathcal{F}$ear often comes when we have
the most to gain, because that's when we
also have the most to lose.

WINTER IS NOT FOREVER PP. 30-33

*Fear took hold upon them there, and pain, as of
a woman in travail.... For this God is our God for ever
and ever: he will be our guide even unto death.*

PSALM 48:6,14

March 24

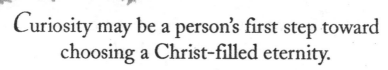

Curiosity may be a person's first step toward choosing a Christ-filled eternity.

LOVE'S ABIDING JOY PP. 199,200

And the keeper of the prison...said, Sirs, what must I do to be saved?

ACTS 16:27,30

~~~~~~~~~~~~~~~~~~~~~~~~~~~~~~

October 9

A family is God's wall
of protection around children.

WINTER IS NOT FOREVER PP. 30-33

Keep me as the apple of the eye,
hide me under the shadow of thy wings.

PSALM 17:8

~~~~~~~~~~~~~~~~

March 25

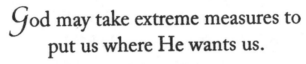

$\mathcal{G}$od may take extreme measures to
put us where He wants us.

LOVE'S ABIDING JOY PP. 195,196

The Midianites sold [Joseph] into Egypt....
And Pharaoh said unto Joseph...only in the throne
will I be greater than thou.

GENESIS 37:24,36;41:39,40

~~~~~~~~~~~~~~~~~~~~~~~~~~~~~

October 8

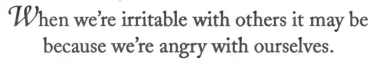

*W*hen we're irritable with others it may be because we're angry with ourselves.

WINTER IS NOT FOREVER P. 17

He that is slow to anger is better than the mighty; and he that ruleth his spirit than he that taketh a city.

PROVERBS 16:32

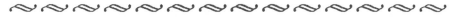

March 26

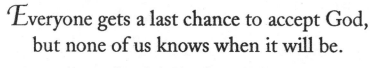

*E*veryone gets a last chance to accept God,
but none of us knows when it will be.

LOVE'S ABIDING JOY P. 186

Now is the accepted time.... Now is the day of salvation.

2 CORINTHIANS 6:2

∾∾∾∾∾∾∾∾∾∾∾∾∾∾∾∾

October 7

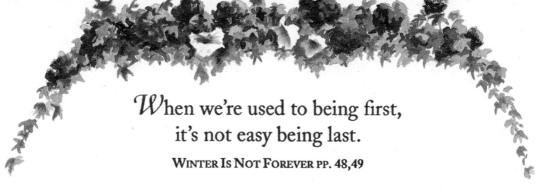

*W*hen we're used to being first,
it's not easy being last.

WINTER IS NOT FOREVER PP. 48,49

*So the last shall be first, and the first last:
for many be called, but few chosen.*

MATTHEW 20:16

~~~~~~~~~~~~~~~~

March 27

$\mathcal{W}$hen it comes to faith, it takes a combination of both working at it, and receiving it as a gift.

LOVE'S ABIDING JOY PP. 178,179

Through faith [they] subdued kingdoms,
wrought righteousness, obtained promises,
stopped the mouths of lions....

HEBREWS 11:33

October 6

*H*aving wrestled with a difficult decision,
we will have more strength for the next one.

WINTER IS NOT FOREVER PP. 49,50

*I will go in the strength of the Lord God: I will make
mention of thy righteousness, even of thine only.*

PSALM 71:16

∽∽∽∽∽∽∽∽∽∽∽∽∽∽∽∽∽

March 28

*W*hen we push people to make
important decisions, we may unwittingly
encourage them to make the wrong one.

LOVE'S ABIDING JOY PP. 177,178

He that is hasty of spirit exalteth folly.

PROVERBS 14:29

~~~~~~~~~~~~~~~~~~~~

October 5

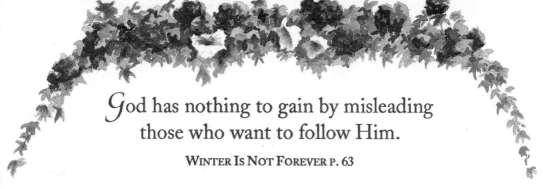

God has nothing to gain by misleading
those who want to follow Him.

WINTER IS NOT FOREVER P. 63

Lead me in thy truth, and teach me:
for thou art the God of my salvation;
on thee do I wait all the day.

PSALM 25:5

~~~~~~~~~~~~~~~~~~~~~~~~~~~~~

March 29

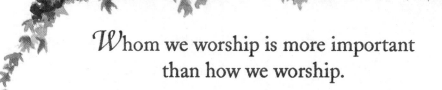

*W*hom we worship is more important
than how we worship.

LOVE'S ABIDING JOY PP. 173,174

Thou shalt have no other gods before me.

EXODUS 20:3

~~~~~~~~~~~~~~~~~~~~

October 4

*Therefore encourage one another
and build each other up.*

1 Thessalonians 5:11 NIV

~~~~~~~~~~~~~~~~~~~~~~~~~~~~~

March 30

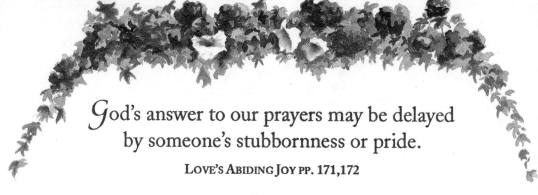

God's answer to our prayers may be delayed
by someone's stubbornness or pride.

LOVE'S ABIDING JOY PP. 171,172

Pride compasseth them about as a chain.

PSALM 73:6

October 3

And let us consider one another to provoke unto love and to good works.

HEBREWS 10:24

≈≈≈≈≈≈≈≈≈≈≈≈≈≈≈≈

March 31

Whenever anything bad happens we can start
watching to see how God will use it for good.

LOVE'S ABIDING JOY PP. 157,158

All things work together for good to them that love God,
to them who are the called according to his purpose.

ROMANS 8:28

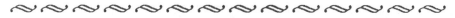

October 2

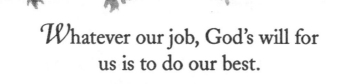

*W*hatever our job, God's will for
us is to do our best.

WINTER IS NOT FOREVER P. 63

And whatsoever ye do in word or deed,
do all in the name of the Lord Jesus, giving thanks
to God and the Father by him.

COLOSSIANS 3:17

~~~~~~~~~~~~~~~~~~~~~~~~

April 1

A miraculously healed body lasts for a lifetime;
a miraculously healed soul lasts for eternity.

LOVE'S ABIDING JOY PP. 154,155

*The water that I shall give him shall be in him a well
of water springing up into everlasting life.*

JOHN 4:14

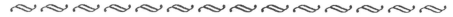

October 1

If we use our authority to walk on people,
we can't expect them to stand on their own two feet.

WINTER IS NOT FOREVER PP. 68,69

*As an eagle stirreth up her nest, fluttereth over her
young, spreadeth abroad her wings, taketh them, beareth
them on her wings: So the Lord alone did lead him,
and there was no strange god with him.*

DEUTERONOMY 32:11,12

April 2

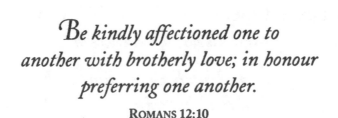

*Be kindly affectioned one to
another with brotherly love; in honour
preferring one another.*

ROMANS 12:10

～～～～～～～～～～～～～～～～～

September 30

If we try to possess another person,
God is not in possession of us.

WINTER IS NOT FOREVER P. 70

Not lording it over those entrusted to you, but being examples to the flock.

1 PETER 5:3 NIV

∾ ∾ ∾ ∾ ∾ ∾ ∾ ∾ ∾ ∾ ∾ ∾ ∾ ∾

April 3

*Lay not up for yourselves treasures
upon earth...but lay up for yourselves treasures
in heaven.... For where your treasure is,
there will your heart be also.*

MATTHEW 6:19-21

∾∾∾∾∾∾∾∾∾∾∾∾∾∾∾∾

September 29

If we get God's approval daily, we don't have to fear His disapproval in the future.

WINTER IS NOT FOREVER P. 73

Study to show thyself approved unto God, a workman that needeth not to be ashamed.

2 TIMOTHY 2:15

~~~~~~~~~~~~~~~~~~~~~~~~~~~~

April 4

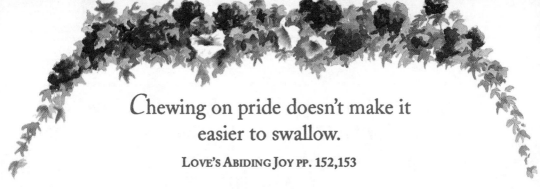

Chewing on pride doesn't make it
easier to swallow.

LOVE'S ABIDING JOY PP. 152,153

In the mouth of the foolish is a rod of pride.

PROVERBS 14:3

~ ~ ~ ~ ~ ~ ~ ~ ~ ~ ~ ~ ~ ~ ~ ~

September 28

Things that cause us grief can be beautiful
if we look at them from the right perspective—
with our faces turned upward.

WINTER IS NOT FOREVER P. 79

And let the beauty of the Lord our God be upon us: and
establish thou the work of our hands upon us; yea, the
work of our hands establish thou it.

PSALM 90:17

April 5

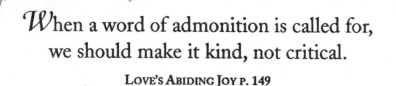

*W*hen a word of admonition is called for,
we should make it kind, not critical.

LOVE'S ABIDING JOY P. 149

A word fitly spoken is like apples of gold.

PROVERBS 25:11

~~~~~~~~~~~~~~~~~~

September 27

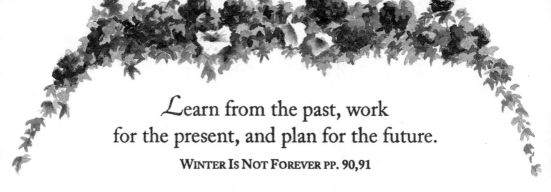

$\mathcal{L}$earn from the past, work
for the present, and plan for the future.

WINTER IS NOT FOREVER PP. 90,91

Go to the ant, thou slugggard;
consider her ways, and be wise.

PROVERBS 6:6

∽∽∽∽∽∽∽∽∽∽∽∽∽∽∽∽∽

$\mathcal{A}$pril 6

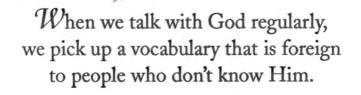

*W*hen we talk with God regularly,
we pick up a vocabulary that is foreign
to people who don't know Him.

LOVE'S ABIDING JOY PP. 147,148

All that heard [Jesus] were astonished at
his understanding and answers.

LUKE 2:47

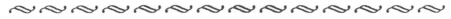

September 26

Giving ourselves is the most costly gift,
and the most valuable.

LOVE'S ABIDING JOY P. 21

This is my body which is given for you.

LUKE 22:19

∾∾∾∾∾∾∾∾∾∾∾∾∾∾∾∾∾∾∾

April 7

The only safe way to walk into the future
is with Someone who has already been there.

LOVE'S ABIDING JOY PP. 140,141

*I am Alpha and Omega, the beginning
and the ending, saith the Lord, which is, and
which was, and which is to come.*

REVELATION 1:8

~~~~~~~~~~~~~~~~~~~~~~~~~~~~~~~~

September 25

If we selfishly consume all the good fruit God produces in our lives, we'll have only inferior seed to plant in the future.

WINTER IS NOT FOREVER PP. 92,93

Sow to yourselves in righteousness, reap in mercy; break up your fallow ground: for it is time to seek the Lord, till he come and rain righteousness upon you.

HOSEA 10:12

~~~~~~~~~~~~~~~~~

April 8

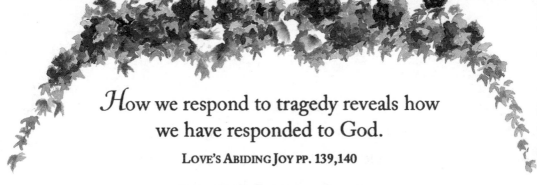

*H*ow we respond to tragedy reveals how
we have responded to God.

LOVE'S ABIDING JOY PP. 139,140

*Then said [Job's] wife unto him,...Curse God
and die.... In all this Job did not sin.*

JOB 2:9,10

∾ ∾ ∾ ∾ ∾ ∾ ∾ ∾ ∾ ∾ ∾ ∾ ∾ ∾ ∾

September 24

$\mathcal{A}$ bad influence is a good thing to avoid.

WINTER IS NOT FOREVER PP. 98,99

Whoso causeth the righteous to go astray in an evil way,
he shall fall himself into his own pit: but the upright
shall have good things in possession.

PROVERBS 28:10

∾∾∾∾∾∾∾∾∾∾∾∾∾∾∾∾∾

April 9

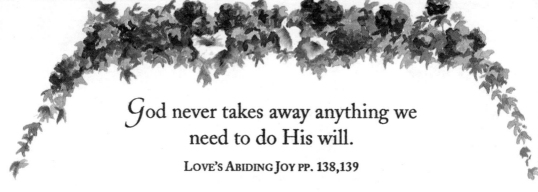

God never takes away anything we
need to do His will.

LOVE'S ABIDING JOY PP. 138,139

*Look to yourselves, that we lose
not those things which we have wrought,
but that we receive a full reward.*

2 JOHN 8

≈ ≈ ≈ ≈ ≈ ≈ ≈ ≈ ≈ ≈ ≈ ≈ ≈ ≈ ≈ ≈

September 23

*I*t is difficult to keep a home
together without love, and true love is
impossible without God.

WINTER IS NOT FOREVER PP. 99,100

Who shall separate us from the love of Christ?
shall tribulation, or distress, or persecution, or famine,
or nakedness, or peril, or sword?

ROMANS 8:35

~~~~~~~~~~~~~~~~~~~~~~~~

April 10

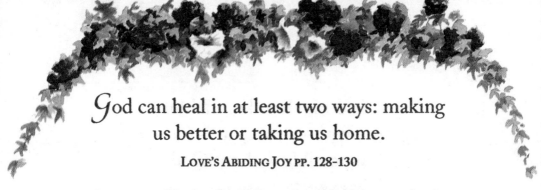

$\mathcal{G}$od can heal in at least two ways: making
us better or taking us home.

LOVE'S ABIDING JOY PP. 128-130

*So now, Christ shall be magnified in my body,
whether it be by life, or by death.*

PHILIPPIANS 1:20

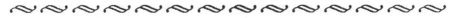

September 22

If answered prayer surprises us,
our praying is more wishing than believing.

WINTER IS NOT FOREVER PP. 105,106

And this is the confidence that we have in him, that,
if we ask any thing according to his will, he heareth us.

1 JOHN 5:14

≈≈≈≈≈≈≈≈≈≈≈≈≈≈≈

April 11

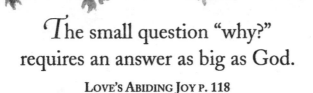

The small question "why?"
requires an answer as big as God.

LOVE'S ABIDING JOY P. 118

My God, my God, why hast thou forsaken me?

MATTHEW 27:46

～～～～～～～～～～～～～～～～

September 21

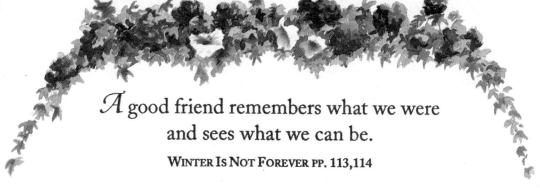

A good friend remembers what we were
and sees what we can be.

WINTER IS NOT FOREVER PP. 113,114

*Iron sharpeneth iron; so a man sharpeneth
the countenance of his friend.*

PROVERBS 27:17

~~~~~~~~~~~~~~~~~~~~~~~

April 12

Blessings sometimes show up in
unrecognizable disguises.

LOVE'S ABIDING JOY PP. 113,114

The LORD thy God turned the curse into a blessing.

DEUTERONOMY 23:5

∾∾∾∾∾∾∾∾∾∾∾∾∾∾∾∾

September 20

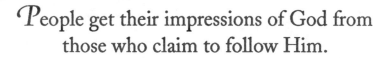

People get their impressions of God from
those who claim to follow Him.

WINTER IS NOT FOREVER P. 125

Be ye followers of me, even as I also am of Christ.

1 CORINTHIANS 11:1

≈≈≈≈≈≈≈≈≈≈≈≈≈≈≈

April 13

If all we do in prayer is tell God what we want, we reduce Him to the role of servant and elevate ourselves to the position of master.

LOVE'S ABIDING JOY P. 111

[Jesus]...prayed, saying, O my Father, if it be possible, let this cup pass from me: nevertheless not as I will, but as thou wilt.

MATTHEW 26:39

September 19

The fear of death can lead to everlasting life.

WINTER IS NOT FOREVER PP. 125,126

He that believeth on the Son hath everlasting life:
and he that believeth not the Son shall not see life;
but the wrath of God abideth on him.

JOHN 3:36

∽∽∽∽∽∽∽∽∽∽∽∽∽∽∽∽

April 14

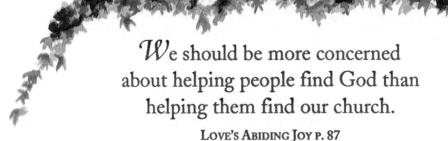

*W*e should be more concerned
about helping people find God than
helping them find our church.

LOVE'S ABIDING JOY P. 87

Those that seek me early shall find me.

PROVERBS 8:17

September 18

God doesn't mind us asking "why," but we don't always understand His answer right away.

LOVE'S ENDURING PROMISE PP. 32,33

My God, my God, why hast thou forsaken me?...
He is not here: for he is risen.

MATTHEW 27:46;28:6

≈≈≈≈≈≈≈≈≈≈≈≈≈≈≈≈≈

April 15

One of the best parts of growing old
is enjoying all the pleasant memories we've
taken time to store up.

LOVE'S ABIDING JOY P. 77

The righteous...shall still bring forth fruit in old age.

PSALM 92:12,14

~~~~~~~~~~~~~~~~~

September 17

$\mathcal{W}$hen there's no way out of a situation,
plow right through it.

WINTER IS NOT FOREVER PP. 133,134

*I go in unto the king, which is not according
to the law: and if I perish, I perish.*

ESTHER 4:16

April 16

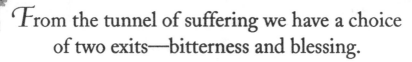

From the tunnel of suffering we have a choice
of two exits—bitterness and blessing.

LOVE'S ABIDING JOY PP. 75,76

*For our...affliction...worketh for us a far more
exceeding and eternal weight of glory.*

2 CORINTHIANS 4:17

September 16

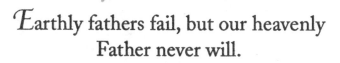

Earthly fathers fail, but our heavenly
Father never will.

WINTER IS NOT FOREVER PP. 146,147

*Behold, what manner of love the Father
hath bestowed upon us, that we should be called the
sons of God: therefore the world knoweth us not,
because it knew him not.*

1 JOHN 3:1

～～～～～～～～～～～～～～～～～

April 17

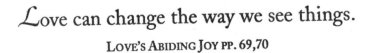

$\mathcal{L}$ove can change the way we see things.

LOVE'S ABIDING JOY PP. 69,70

We look not at the things which are seen,
but at the things which are not seen: for the things
which are seen are temporal; but the things
which are not seen are eternal.

2 CORINTHIANS 4:18

∽∽∽∽∽∽∽∽∽∽∽∽∽∽

September 15

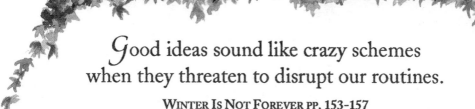

*G*ood ideas sound like crazy schemes
when they threaten to disrupt our routines.

WINTER IS NOT FOREVER PP. 153-157

There are many devices in a man's heart;
nevertheless the counsel of the Lord, that shall stand.

PROVERBS 19:21

❧ ❧ ❧ ❧ ❧ ❧ ❧ ❧ ❧ ❧ ❧ ❧ ❧

April 18

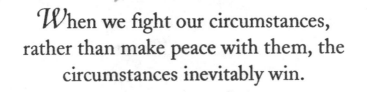

*W*hen we fight our circumstances,
rather than make peace with them, the
circumstances inevitably win.

LOVE'S ABIDING JOY PP. 59, 60

Wait on the LORD: be of good courage,
and he shall strengthen thine heart.

PSALM 27:14

≈≈≈≈≈≈≈≈≈≈≈≈≈≈≈≈≈

September 14

*G*od is big enough to handle small problems.

WINTER IS NOT FOREVER PP. 166,167

Thou hast been my defense and refuge
in the day of my trouble.

PSALM 59:16

~~~~~~~~~~~~~~~~~~~~

April 19

Rest restores our strength;
laziness diminishes it.

WINTER IS NOT FOREVER P. 92

*Rest in the Lord, and wait patiently for him: fret not
thyself because of him who prospereth in his way, because
of the man who bringeth wicked devices to pass.*

PSALM 37:7

~~~~~~~~~~~~~~~~~

September 13

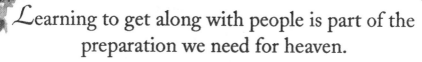

$\mathcal{L}$earning to get along with people is part of the
preparation we need for heaven.

WINTER IS NOT FOREVER PP. 168,169

*By pride cometh contention: but with
the well advised is wisdom.*

PROVERBS 13:10

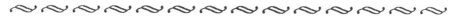

April 20

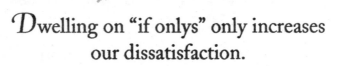

$\mathcal{D}$welling on "if onlys" only increases
our dissatisfaction.

LOVE'S ABIDING JOY PP. 13,14

*Then said Martha unto Jesus, Lord, if thou hadst
been here, my brother had not died.*

JOHN 11:21

~~~~~~~~~~~~~~~~~

September 12

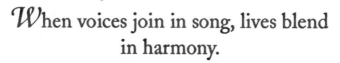

*W*hen voices join in song, lives blend
in harmony.

WINTER IS NOT FOREVER PP. 181,182

*Praise ye the Lord. Sing unto the Lord a new song,
and his praise in the congregation of saints.*

PSALM 149:1

≈≈≈≈≈≈≈≈≈≈≈≈≈≈≈≈≈

April 21

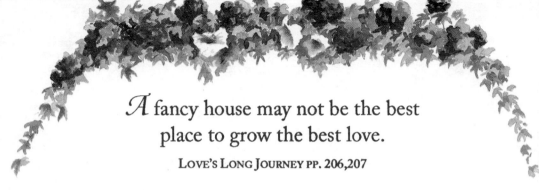

$\mathcal{A}$ fancy house may not be the best
place to grow the best love.

LOVE'S LONG JOURNEY PP. 206,207

The house of the righteous shall stand.

PROVERBS 12:7

~~~~~~~~~~~~~~~~~~~~~~~~~~

September 11

*I*mpatience can cause
wise people to do foolish things.

WINTER IS NOT FOREVER PP. 182,183

But thou, O man of God, flee these things;
and follow after righteousness, godliness, faith,
love, patience, meekness.

1 TIMOTHY 6:11

≈≈≈≈≈≈≈≈≈≈≈≈≈≈≈≈≈

April 22

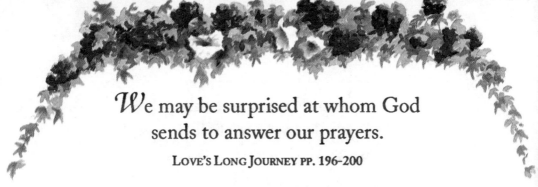

*W*e may be surprised at whom God
sends to answer our prayers.

LOVE'S LONG JOURNEY PP. 196-200

Some have entertained angels unawares.

HEBREWS 13:2

~~~~~~~~~~~~~~~~~~~~~~~~

September 10

The only good reason for making lots
of money is to give it away.

WINTER IS NOT FOREVER PP. 192-194

Charge them that are rich in this
world, that they...do good, that they be rich
in good works, ready to distribute.

1 TIMOTHY 6:17,18

April 23

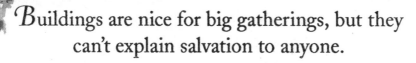

$\mathcal{B}$uildings are nice for big gatherings, but they can't explain salvation to anyone.

LOVE'S LONG JOURNEY PP. 190,191

In the name of our Lord Jesus Christ...
ye are gathered together.

1 CORINTHIANS 5:4

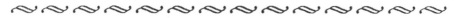

September 9

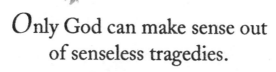

*O*nly God can make sense out
of senseless tragedies.

WINTER IS NOT FOREVER PP. 205,206

For my thoughts are not your thoughts,
neither are your ways my ways, saith the Lord.
For as the heavens are higher than the earth,
so are my ways higher than your ways.

ISAIAH 55:8,9

～～～～～～～～～～～～～～～～～

April 24

A house can keep bad weather out, but only
a home can keep people in.

LOVE'S LONG JOURNEY PP. 186,187

The LORD hath brought me home.

RUTH 1:21

≈≈≈≈≈≈≈≈≈≈≈≈≈≈≈≈≈

September 8

What belongs to God, we can never really lose.

WINTER IS NOT FOREVER PP. 207,208

Blessed be God, even the Father of our Lord Jesus Christ, the Father of mercies, and the God of all comfort; who comforteth us in all our tribulation.

2 CORINTHIANS 1:3,4

∽∽∽∽∽∽∽∽∽∽∽∽∽∽∽∽

April 25

People we can pray with make the best friends.

LOVE'S LONG JOURNEY PP. 165,166

Many were gathered together praying.

ACTS 12:12

～～～～～～～～～～～～～～～

September 7

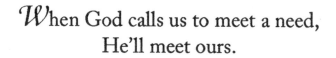

*W*hen God calls us to meet a need,
He'll meet ours.

WINTER IS NOT FOREVER P. 209

I have chosen you, and ordained you,
that ye should go and bring forth fruit, and
that your fruit should remain.

JOHN 15:16

April 26

Only God can keep all His promises.

LOVE'S LONG JOURNEY PP. 152,153

There hath not failed one word
of all his good promise.

1 KINGS 8:56

September 6

The task of every believer is to fight
the effects of sin in the world.

WINTER IS NOT FOREVER P. 216

*Defend the poor and fatherless: do justice to
the afflicted and needy. Deliver the poor and needy:
rid them out of the hand of the wicked.*

PSALM 82:3,4

~ ~ ~ ~ ~ ~ ~ ~ ~ ~ ~ ~ ~ ~ ~ ~ ~

April 27

$\mathcal{A}$ccepting the truth is easier than living a lie.

LOVE'S LONG JOURNEY PP. 151,152

We have a good conscience, in all things
willing to live honestly.

HEBREWS 13:18

∾∾∾∾∾∾∾∾∾∾∾∾∾∾∾∾∾

September 5

A small task, done in obedience to God,
is a big accomplishment.

WINTER IS NOT FOREVER PP. 217,218

A certain poor widow...threw in two mites,...
And [Jesus]...saith...this poor widow hath cast more in,
than all they which have cast into the treasury.

MARK 12:42,43

≈≈≈≈≈≈≈≈≈≈≈≈≈≈≈≈

April 28

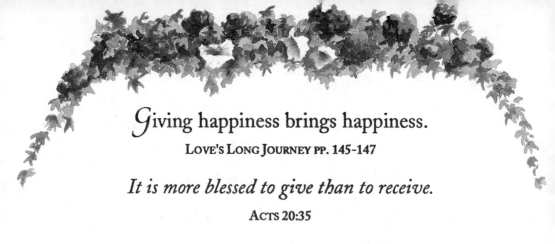

*G*iving happiness brings happiness.

LOVE'S LONG JOURNEY PP. 145-147

It is more blessed to give than to receive.

ACTS 20:35

≈≈≈≈≈≈≈≈≈≈≈≈≈≈≈

September 4

Spiritual maturity, like physical maturity,
brings added responsibility.

SPRING'S GENTLE PROMISE 13,14

Put away childish things....

1 CORINTHIANS 13:11

~~~~~~~~~~~~~~~~~~~~~~~~~

April 29

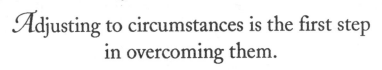

*A*djusting to circumstances is the first step
in overcoming them.

LOVE'S LONG JOURNEY PP. 130-132

I have learned, in whatsoever state I am,
therewith to be content.

PHILIPPIANS 4:11

September 3

Without counsel purposes are disappointed: but in the multitude of counsellors they are established.

PROVERBS 15:22.

~ ~ ~ ~ ~ ~ ~ ~ ~ ~ ~ ~ ~ ~ ~ ~

April 30

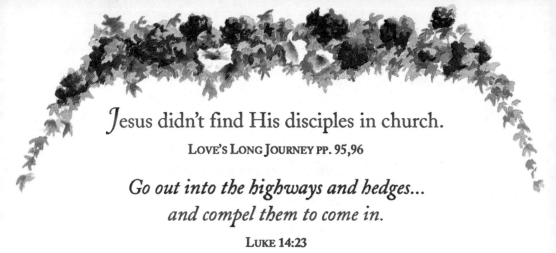

*J*esus didn't find His disciples in church.

LOVE'S LONG JOURNEY PP. 95,96

Go out into the highways and hedges...
and compel them to come in.

LUKE 14:23

≈≈≈≈≈≈≈≈≈≈≈≈≈≈≈≈≈

September 2

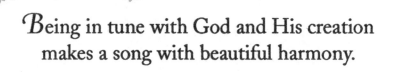

Being in tune with God and His creation
makes a song with beautiful harmony.

SPRING'S GENTLE PROMISE P. 14

I will sing aloud of thy mercy in the morning.

PSALM 59:16

∽∽∽∽∽∽∽∽∽∽∽∽∽∽∽∽

May 1

Reprimands don't always have to be harsh.

LOVE'S LONG JOURNEY P. 92

A soft answer turneth away wrath.

PROVERBS 15:1

∽∽∽∽∽∽∽∽∽∽∽∽∽∽∽

September 1

$\mathcal{P}$raising God for health and prosperity
keeps us from becoming proud.

SPRING'S GENTLE PROMISE P. 18

Forget not all his benefits.

PSALM 103:2

≈≈≈≈≈≈≈≈≈≈≈≈≈≈≈≈

$\mathcal{M}ay$ 2

He that covereth his sins shall not prosper: but whoso confesseth and forsaketh them shall have mercy.

PROVERBS 28:13

~~~~~~~~~~~~~~~~~~~~~~~~~~~

August 31

For thousands of years God has been
working to undo the damage Abraham caused
when he tried to help God.

SPRING'S GENTLE PROMISE PP. 29,30

Learn to do well.

ISAIAH 1:17

~~~~~~~~~~~~~~~~~~~~~~~~

May 3

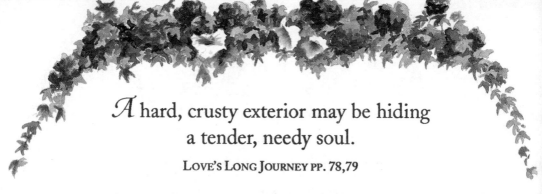

A hard, crusty exterior may be hiding
a tender, needy soul.

LOVE'S LONG JOURNEY PP. 78,79

And Peter remembered the words of Jesus....
And he went out, and wept bitterly.

MATTHEW 26:75

~ ~ ~ ~ ~ ~ ~ ~ ~ ~ ~ ~ ~ ~ ~

August 30

God gives more than we need so we
can give to those in need.

SPRING'S GENTLE PROMISE P. 37

He that hath a bountiful eye shall be blessed;
for he giveth of his bread to the poor.

PROVERBS 22:9

∾∾∾∾∾∾∾∾∾∾∾∾∾∾

May 4

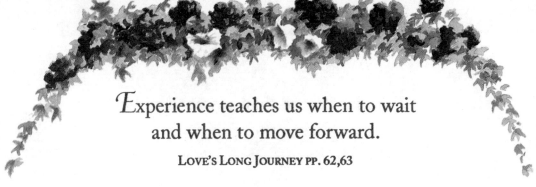

$\mathcal{E}$xperience teaches us when to wait
and when to move forward.

LOVE'S LONG JOURNEY PP. 62,63

I have learned by experience that the LORD
hath blessed me for thy sake.

GENESIS 30:27

❧❧❧❧❧❧❧❧❧❧❧❧❧❧❧

August 29

When we only want what we need, we are on
the right road to spiritual maturity.

SPRING'S GENTLE PROMISE PP. 37,38

*Delight thyself also in the Lord: and he shall
give thee the desires of thine heart.*

PSALM 37:4

~~~~~~~~~~~~~~~~~~~~~~~~~~~~

May 5

*W*orrying about possible adversity is a waste of energy; but preparing for it is not.

LOVE'S LONG JOURNEY PP. 57,58

*Gather all the food...[or] store...against
the seven years of famine.*

GENESIS 41:35,36

August 28

Being the best we can be doesn't require
having the best the world can make.

SPRING'S GENTLE PROMISE PP. 38,39

*If therefore ye have not been faithful
in the unrighteous mammon, who will commit
to your trust the true riches?*

LUKE 16:11

~~~~~~~~~~~~~~~~~~~~

May 6

Trying to spare someone the worry
of knowing the truth may cause them more
worry about what's NOT true.

LOVE'S LONG JOURNEY PP. 53,54

I have not concealed...thy truth.

PSALM 40:10

≈≈≈≈≈≈≈≈≈≈≈≈≈≈≈≈≈

August 27

*W*hat we value reveals how valuable
we are to God.

SPRING'S GENTLE PROMISE PP. 42,43

*Charge them that...they...not...trust
in uncertain riches, but in the living God.*

1 TIMOTHY 6:17

~~~~~~~~~~~~~~~~~~~~~~~

May 7

*W*aiting for the "right time" may be an excuse
for doing the "wrong thing."

LOVE'S LONG JOURNEY P. 49

And [Jesus] said..."Follow me." But he said,
"Lord, suffer me first to go and bury my father."

LUKE 9:59

∾ ∾ ∾ ∾ ∾ ∾ ∾ ∾ ∾ ∾ ∾ ∾ ∾ ∾ ∾

August 26

*W*anting what our peers want is jealousy;
wanting what God wants is righteousness.

SPRING'S GENTLE PROMISE PP. 71,72

*Walk in the Spirit, and ye shall not
fulfill the lust of the flesh.*

GALATIANS 5:16

≈≈≈≈≈≈≈≈≈≈≈≈≈≈≈≈

May 8

Busyness is an ally when it keeps away pain, but it is an enemy when it keeps us away from God.

LOVE'S LONG JOURNEY P. 48

Martha was cumbered about much serving.... Jesus said..."Martha, thou art careful and troubled about many things: but one thing is needful: and Mary hath chosen that good part."

LUKE 10:39-42

August 25

The right mate is worth the wait.

SPRING'S GENTLE PROMISE PP. 72,73

And Jacob loved Rachel, and said, I will serve thee
seven years for Rachel thy younger daughter.

GENESIS 29:18

~~~~~~~~~~~~~~~~~~~~~~~~~~~~

May 9

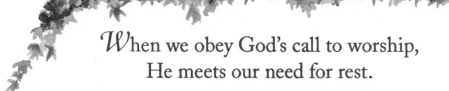

When we obey God's call to worship,
He meets our need for rest.

LOVE'S LONG JOURNEY PP. 45,46

Delight thyself also in the Lord.... Rest in the Lord.

PSALM 37:4,7

≈≈≈≈≈≈≈≈≈≈≈≈≈≈≈

August 24

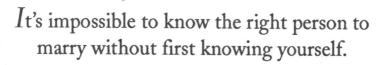

It's impossible to know the right person to
marry without first knowing yourself.

SPRING'S GENTLE PROMISE P. 75

Wise men lay up knowledge.

PROVERBS 10:14

~~~~~~~~~~~~~~~~~~~~~~~~

May 10

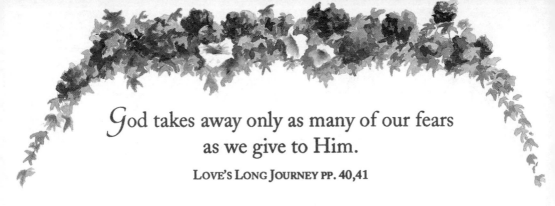

God takes away only as many of our fears
as we give to Him.

LOVE'S LONG JOURNEY PP. 40,41

What time I am afraid, I will trust in thee.

PSALM 56:3

〜〜〜〜〜〜〜〜〜〜〜〜〜〜〜〜〜

August 23

*W*hen we wrap our arms around
those who sorrow, we do so on behalf of Jesus,
who would do it if He were here.

SPRING'S GENTLE PROMISE PP. 81,82

Wherefore comfort one another with these words.

1 THESSALONIANS 4:18

∽∽∽∽∽∽∽∽∽∽∽∽∽∽∽

May 11

*W*hen we let God's Word seep into our lives
little by little, crack by crack, it becomes a part of us.

LOVE'S LONG JOURNEY PP. 21,22

*Man shall...live by...every word that proceedeth
out of the mouth of God.*

MATTHEW 4:4

❧❧❧❧❧❧❧❧❧❧❧❧

August 22

When we lose a person we love,
having something he or she loved can
help ease the pain of loss.

SPRING'S GENTLE PROMISE PP. 86,87

And I will pray the Father, and he shall give you
another Comforter, that he may abide with you for ever.

JOHN 14:16

~~~~~~~~~~~~~~~~~~~~~~~~~~~~~~~

May 12

*G*rowing up doesn't always mean leaving loved ones behind, but it does require leaving some loved things behind. As we take on responsibility, we must give up some of our freedom.

LOVE'S LONG JOURNEY PP. 20,21

But grow up unto him in all things....
Don't give place to the devil.

EPHESIANS 4:15,27

~~~~~~~~~~~~~~~~~~~~~~~~

August 21

Friends may excuse our stupidity;
only God can excuse our sin.

SPRING'S GENTLE PROMISE PP. 98,99

*As far as the east is from the west, so far hath
he removed our transgressions from us.*

PSALM 103:12

∼∼∼∼∼∼∼∼∼∼∼∼∼∼∼

May 13

Judging ourselves by what others think of us is foolish because others know little or nothing about us or our circumstances.

LOVE'S LONG JOURNEY PP. 19,20

Paul thought not good to take him with them....
So Barnabas took Mark.

ACTS 15:38,39

August 20

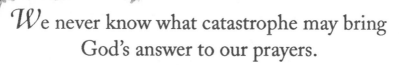

We never know what catastrophe may bring
God's answer to our prayers.

SPRING'S GENTLE PROMISE PP. 98-100

*And suddenly there was a great earthquake...
and every one's bands were loosed.*

ACTS 16:26

∽∽∽∽∽∽∽∽∽∽∽∽∽∽∽∽

May 14

*A*ll the nurturing we do for children and
for each other is for one purpose—
so they'll no longer need us.

LOVE'S ENDURING PROMISE PP. 205,206

We exhorted...you, as a father doth his children,
that ye would walk worthy of God.

1 THESSALONIANS 2:11,12

August 19

*W*hat seems accidental may be providential.

SPRING'S GENTLE PROMISE P. 107

But as for you, ye thought evil against me;
but God meant it unto good.

GENESIS 50:20

~~~~~~~~~~~~~~~~~~~~~~~~

May 15

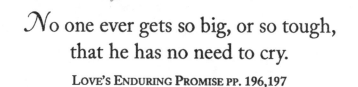

$\mathcal{N}$o one ever gets so big, or so tough,
that he has no need to cry.

LOVE'S ENDURING PROMISE PP. 196, 197

I have heard thy prayer, I have seen thy tears.

2 KINGS 20:5

∾∾∾∾∾∾∾∾∾∾∾∾∾∾∾∾∾

August 18

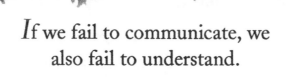

*I*f we fail to communicate, we
also fail to understand.

SPRING'S GENTLE PROMISE PP. 114,115

Let not then your good be evil spoken of.

ROMANS 14:16

≈≈≈≈≈≈≈≈≈≈≈≈≈≈≈≈

May 16

*W*hen everything we have belongs to God we don't have to fret about who's caring for it.

LOVE'S ENDURING PROMISE PP. 193,194

I...know my sheep.... Neither shall any man pluck them out of my hand.

JOHN 10:14,28

August 17

True love is more than sweet nothings.

SPRING'S GENTLE PROMISE PP. 115,116

Whoso findeth a wife findeth a good thing,
and obtaineth favour of the Lord.

PROVERBS 18:22

≈≈≈≈≈≈≈≈≈≈≈≈≈≈≈≈≈

May 17

Our ideas of perfection reveal our real values.

LOVE'S ENDURING PROMISE P. 175

Every man that striveth for the mastery is temperate in all things. Now they do it to obtain a corruptible crown; but we an incorruptible.

1 CORINTHIANS 9:25

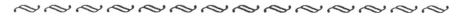

August 16

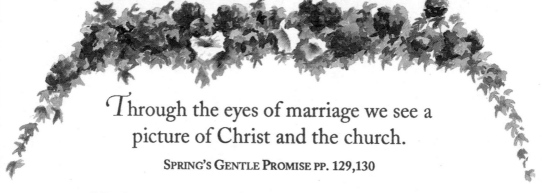

Through the eyes of marriage we see a
picture of Christ and the church.

SPRING'S GENTLE PROMISE PP. 129,130

Husbands, love your wives, even as Christ also
loved the church, and gave himself for it.

EPHESIANS 5:25

~~~~~~~~~~~~~~~~~~~~~~~~~~

May 18

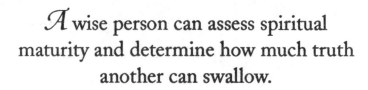

A wise person can assess spiritual
maturity and determine how much truth
another can swallow.

LOVE'S ENDURING PROMISE PP. 170,171

The tongue of the wise useth knowledge aright.

PROVERBS 15:2

≈≈≈≈≈≈≈≈≈≈≈≈≈≈≈≈≈

August 15

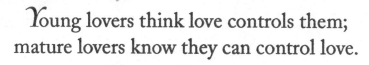

Young lovers think love controls them;
mature lovers know they can control love.

SPRING'S GENTLE PROMISE P. 130

[Love] suffereth long, and is kind.

1 CORINTHIANS 13:4

〜〜〜〜〜〜〜〜〜〜〜〜〜〜〜〜〜〜〜〜〜

May 19

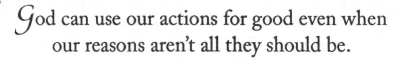

*G*od can use our actions for good even when
our reasons aren't all they should be.

LOVE'S ENDURING PROMISE PP. 167-169

Whether in pretence, or in truth, Christ is preached.

PHILIPPIANS 1:18

∽ ∽ ∽ ∽ ∽ ∽ ∽ ∽ ∽ ∽ ∽ ∽ ∽ ∽ ∽ ∽

August 14

$\mathcal{W}$e'll do better at keeping our earthly accounts balanced if we keep in mind that one day we will have to account to God.

WHEN COMES THE SPRING PP. 131,132

Every one of us shall give account of himself to God.

ROMANS 14:12

≈≈≈≈≈≈≈≈≈≈≈≈≈≈≈≈

May 20

*W*ise words combined with good deeds is the
most effective way to tell others why we love God.

LOVE'S ENDURING PROMISE P. 166

*And whatsoever ye do in word or deed,
do all in the name of the Lord Jesus.*

COLOSSIANS 3:17

∽∽∽∽∽∽∽∽∽∽∽∽∽∽∽∽

August 13

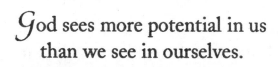

God sees more potential in us
than we see in ourselves.

SPRING'S GENTLE PROMISE P. 136

Ye have not chosen me, but I have chosen you.

JOHN 15:16

~~~~~~~~~~~~~~~~~~~~~~~~

May 21

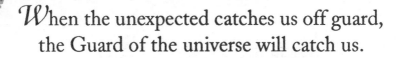

*W*hen the unexpected catches us off guard,
the Guard of the universe will catch us.

LOVE'S ENDURING PROMISE PP. 161,162

*The Lord upholdeth all that fall, and raiseth up
all those that be bowed down.*

PSALM 145:14

≈≈≈≈≈≈≈≈≈≈≈≈≈≈≈≈

August 12

Being right but handling it wrong will make a bad situation worse. Being wrong and handling it right will make a bad situation better.

SPRING'S GENTLE PROMISE PP. 139,140

Wilt thou not cease to pervert the right ways of the Lord?

ACTS 13:10

≈≈≈≈≈≈≈≈≈≈≈≈≈≈≈≈

May 22

The way we choose to go around
an obstacle will determine whether we move
toward God or away from Him.

LOVE'S ENDURING PROMISE P. 146

*Ye did run well; who did hinder you that ye
should not obey the truth?*

GALATIANS 5:7

August 11

*I*t is better to lose our pride than our temper.

SPRING'S GENTLE PROMISE PP. 140,141

Let every man be...slow to wrath.

JAMES 1:19

≈≈≈≈≈≈≈≈≈≈≈≈≈≈≈≈

May 23

$\mathcal{T}$ruth and tears can clear the way to a
deep and lasting friendship.

LOVE'S ENDURING PROMISE PP. 137,138

So Jonathan grieved for David.

1 SAMUEL 20:34

~~~~~~~~~~~~~~~~~~~~~~~~~~

August 10

*O*neness in marriage makes us twice as
strong and half as vulnerable.

SPRING'S GENTLE PROMISE PP. 154,155

For this cause shall a man leave
father and mother, and shall cleave to his wife:
and they twain shall be one flesh.

MATTHEW 19:5

~~~~~~~~~~~~~~~~~~~~~~~~~~~~~

May 24

*A*n education doesn't help us serve God's cause
if it isolates us from those who need Him.

LOVE'S ENDURING PROMISE PP. 134,135

*Where is the wise?... God made foolish
the wisdom of this world.*

1 CORINTHIANS 1:20

~ ~ ~ ~ ~ ~ ~ ~ ~ ~ ~ ~ ~ ~ ~ ~

August 9

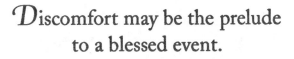

Discomfort may be the prelude
to a blessed event.

SPRING'S GENTLE PROMISE PP. 159,160

*Even we ourselves groan within
ourselves, waiting for the adoption, to wit,
the redemption of our body.*

ROMANS 8:23

$\approx\approx\approx\approx\approx\approx\approx\approx\approx\approx\approx\approx\approx\approx$

May 25

To communicate the Good News,
we need to know more than the "right words";
we need to know the listener.

LOVE'S ENDURING PROMISE PP. 130,131

*I count all things but loss for the excellency
of the knowledge of Christ Jesus.*

PHILIPPIANS 3:8

August 8

*I*f we don't know the suffering
of saying goodbye, we can never know
the joy of saying hello.

SPRING'S GENTLE PROMISE PP. 163,164

Sorrowing most of all for the words which he spake,
that they should see his face no more.

ACTS 20:38

~~~~~~~~~~~~~~~~~~~~~~~~~~~~~~~~

May 26

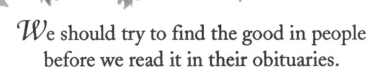

*W*e should try to find the good in people
before we read it in their obituaries.

LOVE'S ENDURING PROMISE P. 124

Whatsoever things...are of a good report...
think on these things.

PHILIPPIANS 4:8

≈≈≈≈≈≈≈≈≈≈≈≈≈≈≈≈

August 7

*S*piritual birth is sometimes
a slow and painful process, but the joy
of conversion makes it worthwhile.

SPRING'S GENTLE PROMISE P. 170

A woman...as soon as she is delivered of the child,
she remembereth no more the anguish, for joy
that a man is born into the world.

JOHN 16:21

May 27

How we pray reveals what we believe.

LOVE'S ENDURING PROMISE PP. 106,107

If we ask any thing according to his will, he heareth us.

1 JOHN 5:14

~~~~~~~~~~~~~~~~~~~~~~

August 6

*W*e need lean times to teach us to lean on God.

SPRING'S GENTLE PROMISE P. 176

And I will restore to you the years that the locust hath
eaten.... And ye shall eat in plenty, and be satisfied,
and praise the name of the Lord your God.

JOEL 2:25,26

~~~~~~~~~~~~~~~~~~~~~~~~~~~~~~~~

May 28

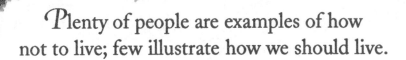

Plenty of people are examples of how
not to live; few illustrate how we should live.

LOVE'S ENDURING PROMISE P. 100

Be thou an example of the believers.

1 TIMOTHY 4:12

~~~~~~~~~~~~~~~~~~~~~~~~~~~~

August 5

People who depend on nature for their livelihood know how dependent they are on God.

SPRING'S GENTLE PROMISE PP. 179,180

Sing unto the Lord with thanksgiving...
who prepareth rain for the earth, who maketh
grass to grow upon the mountains.

PSALM 147:7,8

May 29

Growing spiritually is like growing physically.
Just when we think we've reached a new level of
maturity, we revert to our old, immature behavior.

LOVE'S ENDURING PROMISE PP. 83,84

Simon Peter answered and said, "Thou art the
Christ".... [Peter] denied with an oath.
"I do not know the man."

MATTHEW 16:16; 26:72

~~~~~~~~~~~~~~

August 4

In my Father's house are many mansions....
I go to prepare a place for you. And if I go and prepare
a place for you, I will come again, and receive you unto
myself; that where I am, there ye may be also.

JOHN 14:2,3

∽∽∽∽∽∽∽∽∽∽∽∽∽∽∽∽∽

May 30

Disappointment in adults as well as in children
can lead to bad behavior.

LOVE'S ENDURING PROMISE PP. 82,83

And the soul of the people was much discouraged....
And the people spake against God.

NUMBERS 21:4,5

∽∽∽∽∽∽∽∽∽∽∽∽∽∽∽

August 3

[Love] suffereth long, and is kind; [love] envieth not; love vaunteth not itself, is not puffed up, doth not behave itself unseemly, seeketh not her own.

1 Corinthians 13:4,5

≈≈≈≈≈≈≈≈≈≈≈≈≈≈≈

May 31

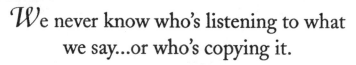

*W*e never know who's listening to what
we say...or who's copying it.

LOVE'S ENDURING PROMISE P. 66

Be ye followers of me, even as I also am of Christ.

1 CORINTHIANS 11:1

∾ ∾ ∾ ∾ ∾ ∾ ∾ ∾ ∾ ∾ ∾ ∾ ∾ ∾ ∾ ∾

August 2

*I*t is just as impossible to survive
without water from heaven as it is to survive
without water from earth.

SPRING'S GENTLE PROMISE P. 183

And the Lord shall guide thee continually,
and satisfy thy soul in drought.

ISAIAH 58:11

∾∾∾∾∾∾∾∾∾∾∾∾∾∾∾∾∾

June 1

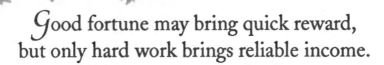

*G*ood fortune may bring quick reward,
but only hard work brings reliable income.

LOVE'S ENDURING PROMISE P. 60

Work with your own hands...
that ye may have lack of nothing.

1 THESSALONIANS 4:11,12

≈≈≈≈≈≈≈≈≈≈≈≈≈≈≈≈

August 1

A taste of what we don't have makes us
discontent with what we do have.

SPRING'S GENTLE PROMISE PP. 184,185

Oh that I were as in months past, as in
the days when God preserved me.

JOB 29:2

≋≋≋≋≋≋≋≋≋≋≋≋≋≋

June 2

*In my Father's house are many mansions....
I go to prepare a place for you. And if I go and prepare a
place for you, I will come again, and receive you unto
myself; that where I am, there ye shall be also.*

JOHN 14:2,3

July 31

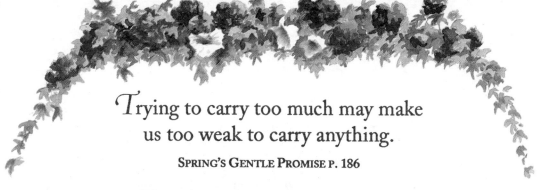

Trying to carry too much may make
us too weak to carry anything.

SPRING'S GENTLE PROMISE P. 186

Therefore take no thought, saying,
What shall we eat? or, What shall we drink?
or, Wherewithal shall we be clothed?

MATTHEW 6:31

∽∾∽∾∽∾∽∾∽∾∽∾∽∾∽∾∽∾∽

June 3

*F*or God so loved the world, that he gave
his only begotten Son, that whosoever believeth in him
should not perish, but have everlasting life.

JOHN 3:16

∽∽∽∽∽∽∽∽∽∽∽∽∽∽∽∽∽∽

July 30

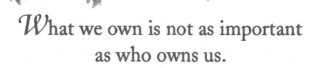

*W*hat we own is not as important
as who owns us.

SPRING'S GENTLE PROMISE PP. 195,196

*For your heavenly Father knoweth that
ye have need of all these things.*

MATTHEW 6:32

≈≈≈≈≈≈≈≈≈≈≈≈≈≈≈≈≈

June 4

$\mathcal{D}$oing right is one decision we can make
without considering the consequences.

LOVE'S ENDURING PROMISE PP. 58,59

As for the pure, his work is right.

PROVERBS 21:8

≈≈≈≈≈≈≈≈≈≈≈≈≈≈

July 29

*W*hen our strength wanes, God's remains.

SPRING'S GENTLE PROMISE PP. 202,203

My grace is sufficient for thee: for my strength is made perfect in weakness.

2 CORINTHIANS 12:9

June 5

*W*hether or not God will answer
our prayers is not a matter of question, but HOW
He will answer may leave us wondering.

LOVE'S ENDURING PROMISE P. 54

The eyes of the Lord are over the righteous,
and his ears are open unto their prayers.

1 PETER 3:12

∽∽∽∽∽∽∽∽∽∽∽∽∽∽∽∽∽

July 28

*W*hen the end is near, so is God.

SPRING'S GENTLE PROMISE P. 203

Thou art near, O Lord.

PSALM 119:151

~~~~~~~~~~~~~~~~~~~~~~~~~

June 6

Stubbornness and selfishness
go hand in hand. People who have one
almost always have the other.

LOVE'S ENDURING PROMISE P. 50

Stubbornness is as iniquity and idolatry.

1 SAMUEL 15:23

~~~~~~~~~~~~~~~~~~~~~~~~

July 27

When we don't see God working,
we're looking in the wrong place.

SPRING'S GENTLE PROMISE P. 205

*Because that, when they knew God, they glorified
him not as God, neither were thankful.*

ROMANS 1:21

∽∽∽∽∽∽∽∽∽∽∽∽∽∽∽∽

June 7

The ability to share a person's grief is a gift from God, but a painful one to accept.

LOVE'S ENDURING PROMISE PP. 45,46

Weep with them that weep.

ROMANS 12:15

∽∽∽∽∽∽∽∽∽∽∽∽∽∽∽∽

July 26

God expressed His love for us in
a personal letter that we are to share with
the rest of the world.

SPRING'S GENTLE PROMISE PP. 211, 212

And these things write we unto you,
that your joy may be full.

1 JOHN 1:4

~ ~ ~ ~ ~ ~ ~ ~ ~ ~ ~ ~ ~ ~ ~ ~

June 8

$\mathcal{M}$aturity teaches us the necessity of patience,
but it's still difficult to achieve.

LOVE'S ENDURING PROMISE P. 39

Follow after...patience.

1 TIMOTHY 6:11

~~~~~~~~~~~~~~~~~~~~~~~~

July 25

*W*e give ourselves because He gave Himself.

SPRING'S GENTLE PROMISE PP. 212,213

*And walk in love, as Christ also hath
loved us, and hath given himself for us
an offering and a sacrifice to God.*

EPHESIANS 5:2

∾∾∾∾∾∾∾∾∾∾∾∾∾∾

June 9

God doesn't pry us away from our sins.
He insists that we let go of them ourselves
before He carts them away.

LOVE'S ENDURING PROMISE PP. 33,34

*If we confess our sins, he is faithful
and just to forgive us our sins, and to cleanse
us from all unrighteousness.*

1 JOHN 1:9

July 24

*H*onesty and vulnerability lead to camaraderie.

SPRING'S GENTLE PROMISE P. 213

Wherefore laying aside...all guile, and hypocrisies.

1 PETER 2:1

～～～～～～～～～～～～～～～

June 10

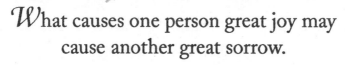

$\mathcal{W}$hat causes one person great joy may
cause another great sorrow.

WINTER IS NOT FOREVER PP. 126-128

*Rejoice with them that do rejoice and
weep with them that weep.*

ROMANS 12:15

∾∾∾∾∾∾∾∾∾∾∾∾∾∾∾

July 23

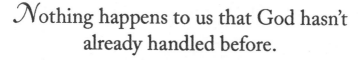

$\mathcal{N}$othing happens to us that God hasn't
already handled before.

SPRING'S GENTLE PROMISE PP. 218,219

*Although the fig tree shall not blossom,
neither shall fruit be in the vine.... Yet I will rejoice
in the Lord, I will joy in the God of my salvation.
The Lord God is my strength.*

HABAKKUK 3:17

~~~~~~~~~~~~~~~~~~~~

$\mathcal{J}$une II

*H*aving nice things doesn't make a person nice.

LOVE'S ENDURING PROMISE PP. 28,29

Covet earnestly the best gifts.

1 CORINTHIANS 12:31

≈≈≈≈≈≈≈≈≈≈≈≈≈≈≈

July 22

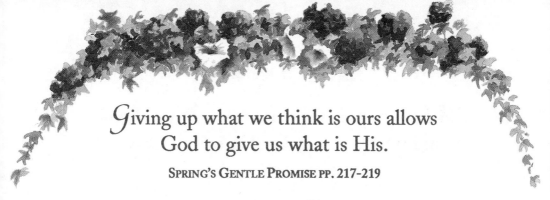

Giving up what we think is ours allows
God to give us what is His.

SPRING'S GENTLE PROMISE PP. 217-219

*Whosoever shall lose his life for my sake...
the same shall save it.*

MARK 8:35

June 12

*W*hen we pray for what we want we should keep in mind that only God knows what we need.

LOVE'S ENDURING PROMISE PP. 24,25

If ye then, being evil, know how to give good gifts unto your children, how much more shall your Father which is in heaven give good things, to them that ask him?

MATTHEW 7:11

≈≈≈≈≈≈≈≈≈≈≈≈≈≈≈≈

July 21

*W*hen God gives us another chance,
there's no risk involved.

SPRING'S GENTLE PROMISE PP. 220-222

*And God appeared unto Jacob again...
and blessed him.*

GENESIS 35:9

June 13

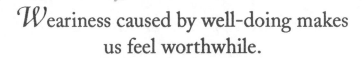

*W*eariness caused by well-doing makes
us feel worthwhile.

LOVE'S ENDURING PROMISE P. 20

Laboring night and day...we preached
unto you the gospel of God.... For what...is our
crown of rejoicing?... Even ye.

1 THESSALONIANS 2:9,19

July 20

Grief is a natural and healthy emotion when a loved one dies, but self-pity helps no one.

LOVE COMES SOFTLY PP. 13,14

Though he cause grief, yet will he have compassion according to the multitude of his mercies.

LAMENTATIONS 3:32

〜〜〜〜〜〜〜〜〜〜〜〜〜〜

June 14

Despite our stubbornness, God does not dismiss us from His thoughts.

WHEN CALLS THE HEART P. 206

Thou compassest my path and my lying down, and art acquainted with all my ways. Thou hast beset me behind and before, and laid thine hand upon me. Such knowledge is too wonderful for me.

PSALM 139:3,5,6

July 19

Though it goes against our senses
to think so, what seems to be a bad alternative
may be the best one.

LOVE COMES SOFTLY PP. 15,16

Return thou.... And Ruth said...
Whither thou goest, I will go.

RUTH 1:16

≈≈≈≈≈≈≈≈≈≈≈≈≈≈≈≈

June 15

*G*etting things accomplished isn't nearly as
important as taking time for love.

LOVE'S ENDURING PROMISE P. 17

By love serve one another.

GALATIANS 5:13

∾ ∾ ∾ ∾ ∾ ∾ ∾ ∾ ∾ ∾ ∾ ∾ ∾ ∾ ∾

July 18

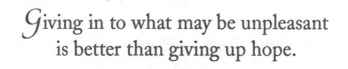

$\mathcal{G}$iving in to what may be unpleasant
is better than giving up hope.

LOVE COMES SOFTLY P. 17

*For to him that is joined to
all the living there is hope: for a living dog
is better than a dead lion.*

ECCLESIASTES 9:4

June 16

God has given us two ways to communicate—
with words and with actions. We need
both to do the job right.

LOVE'S ENDURING PROMISE PP. 12,13

*And when he had thus spoken he showed them his
hands and his feet.... And they worshipped him,
and returned...with great joy.*

LUKE 24:40,52

July 17

The most sensitive response may be silence.

LOVE COMES SOFTLY PP. 18-20

He that refraineth his lips is wise.

PROVERBS 10:19

~~~~~~~~~~~~~~~~~~~~~~~~

June 17

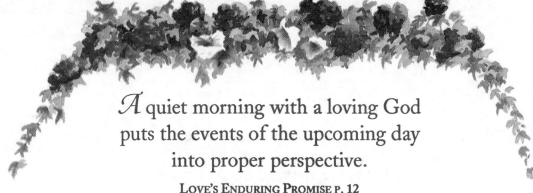

A quiet morning with a loving God
puts the events of the upcoming day
into proper perspective.

LOVE'S ENDURING PROMISE P. 12

Be quiet; fear not.

ISAIAH 7:4

∽∽∽∽∽∽∽∽∽∽∽∽∽∽∽∽

July 16

Being religious doesn't always save us
"a heap of trouble," but it ought to keep us
from causing trouble for others.

LOVE COMES SOFTLY PP. 23,24

In this world you will have trouble.
But take heart! I have overcome the world.

JAMES 1:27

June 18

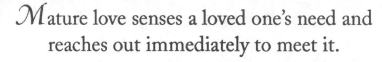

$\mathcal{M}$ature love senses a loved one's need and
reaches out immediately to meet it.

LOVE'S ENDURING PROMISE PP. 9,10

That their hearts might be comforted,
being knit together in love, and unto all riches
of the full assurance of understanding.

COLOSSIANS 2:2

∽∽∽∽∽∽∽∽∽∽∽∽∽∽

July 15

$\mathcal{L}$ove comes when we take the time
to understand and care for another person.

LOVE COMES SOFTLY PP. 25-31

Whosoever shall give to drink unto
one of these little ones a cup of cold water...
shall in no wise lose his reward.

MATTHEW 10:42

∼∼∼∼∼∼∼∼∼∼∼∼∼∼∼∼∼

June 19

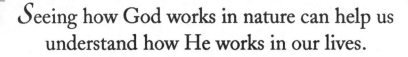

Seeing how God works in nature can help us
understand how He works in our lives.

LOVE COMES SOFTLY PP. 179,180

*For the invisible things of him from the creation
of the world are clearly seen.*

ROMANS 1:20

~ ~ ~ ~ ~ ~ ~ ~ ~ ~ ~ ~ ~ ~ ~

July 14

*W*e can be grateful that God
does indeed know us all by name; we too
need all the help we can get.

LOVE COMES SOFTLY PP. 32,33

*I have called thee by thy name....When thou passest
though the waters, I will be with thee.*

ISAIAH 43:1,2

June 20

Strength comes in quietness.

LOVE COMES SOFTLY P. 179

In quietness and confidence shall be your strength.

ISAIAH 30:15 NIV

∾∾∾∾∾∾∾∾∾∾∾∾∾∾

July 13

$\mathcal{M}$istakes sometimes turn into tragedy, but we
can be grateful that most of the time
our pride is all that gets hurt.

LOVE COMES SOFTLY PP. 38,39

And when they found him not, they turned back....
After three days they found him in the temple...
about [his] Father's business.

LUKE 2:45-49

June 21

*W*hen the question is sorrow,
time will answer it.

LOVE COMES SOFTLY PP. 176,177

Ye shall be sorrowful, but your sorrow
shall be turned into joy.

JOHN 16:20

~~~~~~~~~~~~~~~~~~~~~~~~~~~~

July 12

Sometimes we wish and pray
for what we think will make us happy,
not realizing that we already have it.

LOVE COMES SOFTLY P. 41

The eyes of your understanding being
enlightened; that ye may know...the riches
of the glory of his inheritance.

EPHESIANS 1:18

∽∽∽∽∽∽∽∽∽∽∽∽∽∽∽∽∽∽

June 22

People, like children and seeds,
have unique characteristics that require
special handling and treatment.

LOVE COMES SOFTLY P. 172

O Lord thou has searched me, and known me.
Thou knowest my downsitting and mine uprising,
thou understandest my thought afar off.

PSALM 139:1,2

≈≈≈≈≈≈≈≈≈≈≈≈≈≈≈≈

July 11

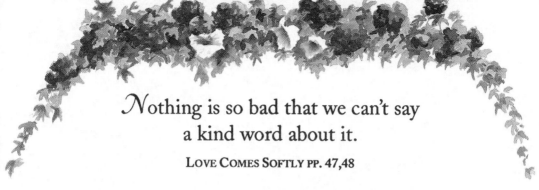

*N*othing is so bad that we can't say
a kind word about it.

LOVE COMES SOFTLY PP. 47,48

*Everything God created is good and...[is to] be
received with thanksgiving.*

1 TIMOTHY 4:4

~~~~~~~~~~~~~~~~~~~~~~~~~~~~~~~~~~

June 23

Sharing God with others, unlike sharing anything else, does not diminish our portion.

LOVE COMES SOFTLY PP. 166,167

Philip findeth Nathanael, and saith unto him, we have found...Jesus.

JOHN 1:45

≈≈≈≈≈≈≈≈≈≈≈≈≈≈≈≈

July 10

A caring heart and a simple deed
can relieve another's grief.

LOVE COMES SOFTLY P. 54

He careth for you.

1 PETER 5:7

~~~~~~~~~~~~~~~~~~~~~~~~~~~~~~~~~~~~~~

June 24

*I*n his graciousness, God gives us
many luxuries; we make a mistake when
we consider them necessities.

LOVE COMES SOFTLY PP. 153-155

*The fowls...do...not gather into barns; yet your
heavenly Father feedeth them.*

MATTHEW 6:26

∽ ∽ ∽ ∽ ∽ ∽ ∽ ∽ ∽ ∽ ∽ ∽ ∽ ∽ ∽ ∽

July 9

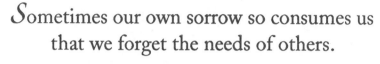

Sometimes our own sorrow so consumes us
that we forget the needs of others.

LOVE COMES SOFTLY PP. 58,59

Look not every man on his own things,
but...also on the things of other.

PHILIPPIANS 2:4

June 25

*W*hen others don't know how
to pray for themselves, God answers our
prayers on their behalf.

LOVE COMES SOFTLY PP. 149,150

Pray for one another.

JAMES 5:16

∽∽∽∽∽∽∽∽∽∽∽∽∽∽∽∽∽

July 8

*W*hen our days are filled with crying,
we can trust that God, in time,
will again bring laughter.

LOVE COMES SOFTLY P. 59

Blessed are ye that weep now: for ye shall laugh.

LUKE 6:21

❧❧❧❧❧❧❧❧❧❧❧❧❧❧❧❧

June 26

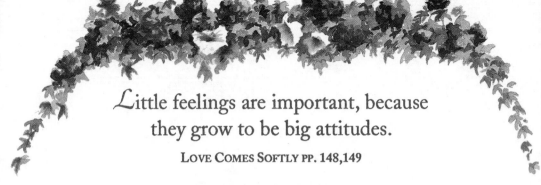

Little feelings are important, because
they grow to be big attitudes.

LOVE COMES SOFTLY PP. 148,149

*Thy servant slew both the lion and the bear: and
this...Philistine shall be as one of them.*

1 SAMUEL 17:36

≈≈≈≈≈≈≈≈≈≈≈≈≈≈≈≈

July 7

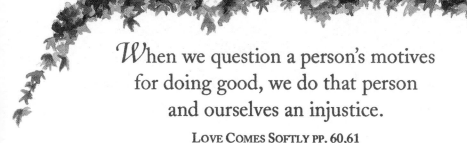

*W*hen we question a person's motives
for doing good, we do that person
and ourselves an injustice.

LOVE COMES SOFTLY PP. 60,61

*Judge not...but consider...the beam
that is in thine own eye.*

MATTHEW 7:1-3

∽∽∽∽∽∽∽∽∽∽∽∽∽∽∽

June 27

It's natural to want to blame something
or someone for bad circumstances, but doing
so only gives us a handle with which to
hang on to bitterness.

LOVE COMES SOFTLY P. 140

Follow peace with all men...lest any root of bitterness
springing up trouble you.

HEBREWS 12:14,15

July 6

$\mathcal{L}$eading people to God by the way
we live, rather than pushing them to acknowledge
Him, can relieve their fear of approaching
Him for the first time.

LOVE COMES SOFTLY P. 82

Ye are our epistle written in our hearts,
known and read of all men.

2 CORINTHIANS 3:2

June 28

*G*od's love doesn't always come
waving flags, either. It too can "steal
up on ya gradual like."

LOVE COMES SOFTLY PP. 136,137

God commendeth his love toward us...
whole we were yet sinners.

ROMANS 5:8

~~~~~~~~~~~~~~~~~~~

July 5

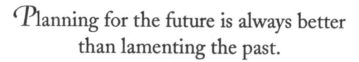

Planning for the future is always better
than lamenting the past.

LOVE COMES SOFTLY PP. 107,108

*For I know the thoughts that I think
toward you...thoughts of peace and not of evil...
to give you hope and a future.*

JEREMIAH 29:11

~~~~~~~~~~~~~~~~~~~~~~~~~~~~~

June 29

Intense pain often precedes immense pleasure.

LOVE COMES SOFTLY PP. 131-133

I take pleasure in infirmities...when I am weak, then am I strong.

2 CORINTHIANS 12:10

∽∽∽∽∽∽∽∽∽∽∽∽∽∽∽∽∽∽∽

July 4

*Ye have received the Spirit of adoption,
whereby we cry, Abba, Father. The Spirit itself
beareth witness with our spirit, that we are the children
of God: And if children, then heirs; heirs of God,
and joint-heirs with Christ.*

ROMANS 8:15-17

~~~~~~~~~~~~~~~~~~~~~~~~~~~~~~~~~~

June 30

*H*aving someone who understands is
a great blessing for ourselves. Being someone who
understands is a great blessing to others.

LOVE COMES SOFTLY P. 116

*We have...an high priest...[that can] be touched
with the feeling of our infirmities.*

HEBREWS 4:15

≈ ≈ ≈ ≈ ≈ ≈ ≈ ≈ ≈ ≈ ≈ ≈ ≈ ≈

July 3

*H*aving something to look forward to can improve our attitude and outlook, and Christians always have something to look forward to.

LOVE COMES SOFTLY PP. 108,109

Looking for...the glorious appearing of...Jesus Christ.

TITUS 2:13

~~~~~~~~~~~~~~~~~~~~~~~~~~~~

July 1

$\mathcal{W}$e defeat only ourselves when we
let circumstances determine our attitude.

LOVE COMES SOFTLY PP. 114,115

*And having food and raiment
let us be therewith content.*

1 TIMOTHY 6:8

July 2